D1549636

THE COMBINATION OVEN COOKBOOK

Dear Microwave Cook

Now that all the advantages a microwave cooker brings to our modern, hectic lifestyle are well established, a combination cooker can overcome the one big drawback of the microwave – the lack of traditional browning. With the advent of combination models, the microwave doubters and sceptics should sit up and take notice!

On the other hand, as confirmed devotees of the microwave cooker, we initially had our own doubts and scepticisms about the combination models – would they really offer any great advantage? But having now mused a while, got to grips with the various accessories and experimented with the different cooking techniques, we find that we have not lost a microwave, but gained a conventional oven! In the combination cookers, the best of both worlds are contained in one appliance, offering the choice of defrosting, reheating or cooking by microwave, cooking by convection, or by combination of the two. In some models grilling is also possible. Different cookers incorporate a selection of various other features and many include microprocessor touch pad electronic controls which are infinitely easier to set than the video!

In this book, Rosemary and I have put together our knowledge of microwave cookers, combination models and many years of experience to produce a selection of combination recipes. We assume that you already have a book on microwave cooking – there are many excellent titles around from which to choose – and we have concentrated on leading you into the world of combination cooking. We feel sure that you will be delighted with the results.

Yours sincerely

Val Collins. Rosemary Moon.

DAVID & CHARLES
Newton Abbot London North Pomfret (Vt)

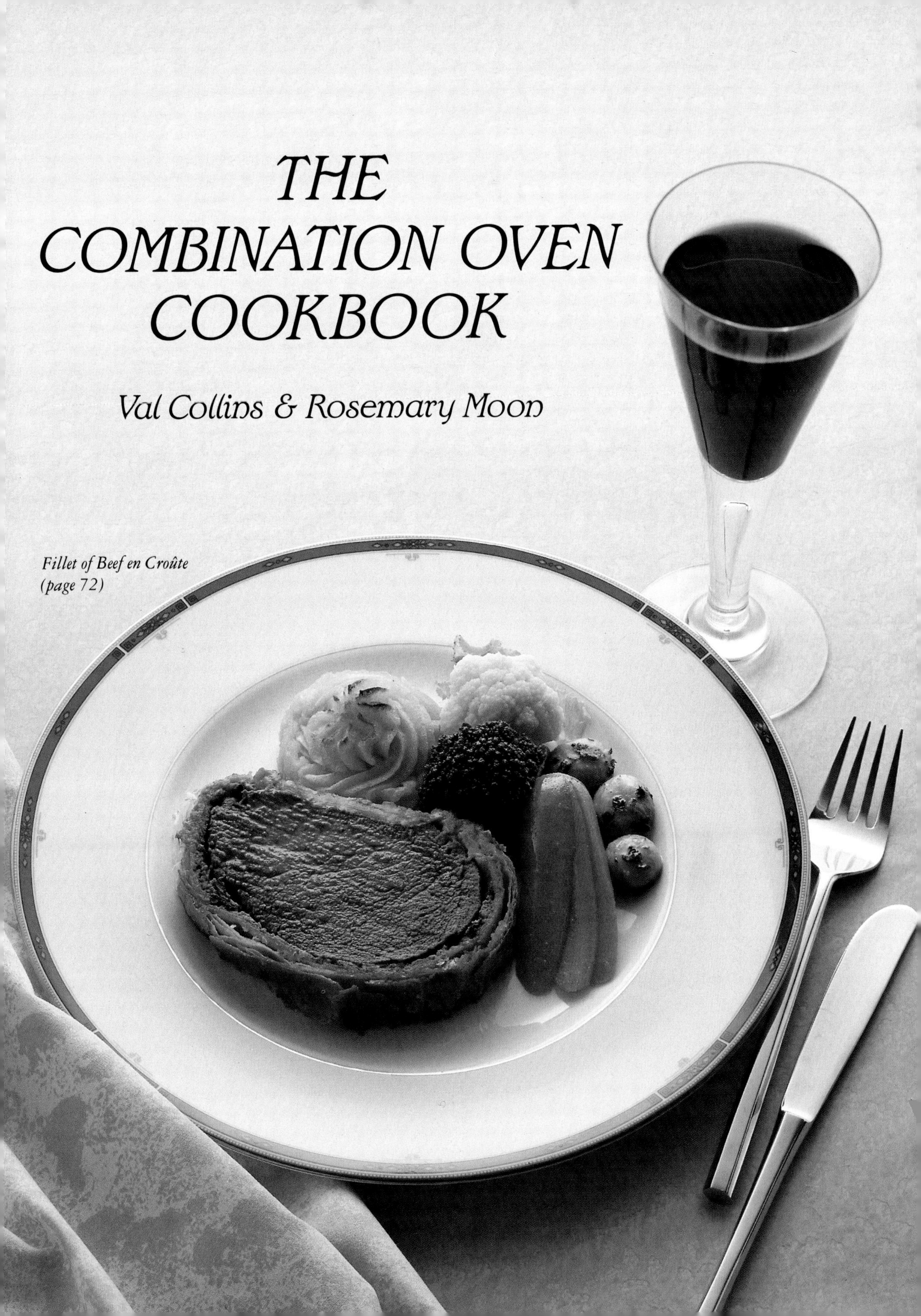

THE COMBINATION OVEN COOKBOOK

Val Collins & Rosemary Moon

Fillet of Beef en Croûte
(page 72)

British Library Cataloguing in Publication Data

Collins, Val
The combination cookbook.
1. Cookery
I. Title II. Moon, Rosemary
641.5 TX717

ISBN 0-7153-9065-1

Phototypeset by Typesetters (Birmingham) Ltd,
Smethwick, West Midlands
and printed in Italy
by New Interlitho, Milan
for David & Charles Publishers plc
Brunel House Newton Abbot Devon

Published in the United States of America
by David & Charles Inc
North Pomfret Vermont 05053 USA

Contents

Introduction

Combination cookers

As the name implies, a combination cooker incorporates more than one cooking method in the same compartment. It is usually larger in size and more expensive than a normal microwave cooker. On occasions, it may be referred to as a multi-function oven, offering the choice of selecting between a minimum of three or sometimes as many as five different cooking modes:

1 Microwave cooking only
2 Convection cooking only
3 Combination of microwave and convection cooking
4 Grilling
5 Combination of grilling and microwave cooking

The advantage of combination oven cooking is that while traditional browning is being achieved from a conventional heat source, at the same time microwave energy is being distributed throughout the oven cavity, speeding up the cooking process. This means that near-traditional results may be obtained in a fraction of the normal cooking time. Although the time savings on combination cooking over conventional methods are not as great as when cooking by microwave alone, the savings are still worthwhile. Depending on what you are cooking, on average as much as 75 per cent can be saved by microwave cooking, whereas combination cooking saves up to 50 per cent but with the advantage that the final result is virtually the same as when cooked conventionally.

The technical details differ between the various manufacturers, but basically the cooking systems fall into one of three groups:

1 Convection heat with pulsed microwave power
2 Convection heat with continuous level microwave power
3 Pulsed convection heat and microwave power

Although some multifunction cookers may offer the choice of more than one type of convection (or conventional) heating in the same oven, the heat source usually falls into one of three categories:

1 *Circulating hot air via an element and fan* which are both usually situated either behind the rear wall or above the roof of the oven. This system provides fast and efficient heating and most cooking can be carried out from a cold start. Some manufacturers may also provide an additional element situated in the top of the compartment which can be used as a grill, but may also provide an additional boost to raise the oven temperature very quickly during the initial cooking time.

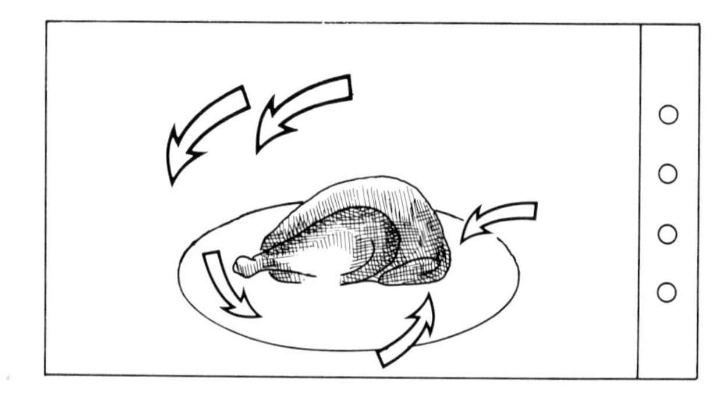

2 *Top and bottom heating elements* which, as the description suggests, are situated in the roof and underneath the base of the oven cavity. This system provides even heating from above and below, but the height for food and dishes may be limited. Although manufacturers suggest cooking can be carried out from a cold start, cooking times may be slightly longer than for a fan convection system. The top element may also be used as a grill in most models with this type of heating.

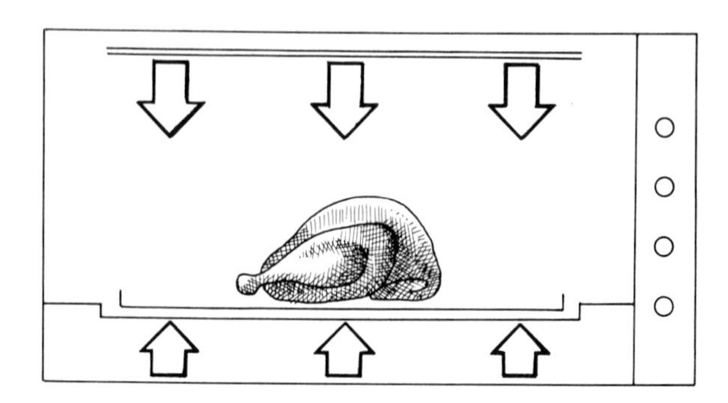

3 *Halogen heat lamps* which give immediate response and fast browning. As the complementary cooking power in a combination cooker, halogen heat is a world first in microwave technology as it offers a neat interior to the oven, free of normal heating elements as the lamps are protected behind smooth glass windows. Halogen heat is essentially a browning device which can also be used for grilling, however it is not temperature controlled as is normal on the other types of combination cookers.

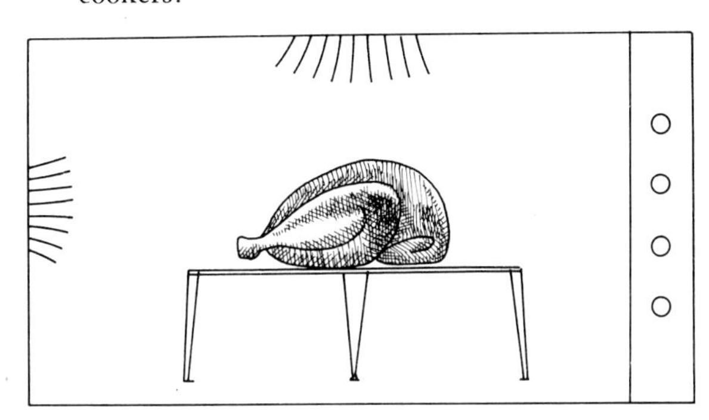

Some combination models incorporate automatic cooking programs which determine the convection temperature and microwave power level depending on the food category selected. All you have to do is program in the weight of the food or the cooking time. Other models give a number of set programs for different food categories where temperatures and microwave power levels are preselected for you. There are one or two models which have just one combination setting with a set microwave power level and oven temperature which limits the types of foods which may be cooked. The remainder leave you the choice of selecting from both a complete range of oven temperatures and two or more microwave power levels to suit various food types.

Most combination cookers come with a variety of cooking accessories, and other features can include automatic defrosting programs, variable microwave power levels, automatic sensor microwave cooking, automatic cooking by weight, programmable multimode facility, automatic delayed start (timer control), or a pyrolitic cleaning cycle (see page 8). A cooling system is usually incorporated to keep both the cabinet and controls to an optimum low temperature level. Some models can be built in to kitchen cabinets – well worth considering if you are short of work surface space.

Accessories

It is important to read the manufacturer's operating instructions and to familiarise yourself with the recommended uses of the accessories supplied with your cooker. It will not take long to get to grips with the different combinations of the racks and trays for various foods and cooking modes and this will help to ensure that the best results are obtained.

The number and type of accessories do vary slightly between the different manufacturers, but basically consist of a metal, ceramic or glass turntable or oven shelf (which, as with all microwave cookers, should always be left in position during cooking), one, two or three cooking racks or trivets, and perhaps a splatter guard or drip tray, a baking tray or plate and a removable handle. Some models allow the turntable to be stopped if required when using the convection mode, enabling larger food items or dishes (which would otherwise not rotate on the turntable) to be cooked.

Low rack

Dishes are placed on the low rack during combination or convection cooking to allow the hot air to circulate all around and underneath the food. Often the low rack is also used for faster and more even microwave cooking – particularly in ovens with metal turntables – to ensure the microwaves can penetrate the base of the dish to cook the food, but do check the manufacturer's recommendations.

Medium rack

The medium rack provides an alternative cooking position in some models to allow certain food types to be positioned closer to elements or halogen heat lamps for browning during combination or convection cooking. A medium/low rack may be the only rack required and supplied in some cookers.

High rack

This can be fitted in conjunction with the low rack for two-level cooking, but is generally used in the convection mode only, otherwise uneven cooking results may occur. It may be necessary to swop food between the racks halfway through cooking or to remove that on the top tray first. The high rack may also be used in some models to position the food closer to the element or halogen heat lamps for grilling.

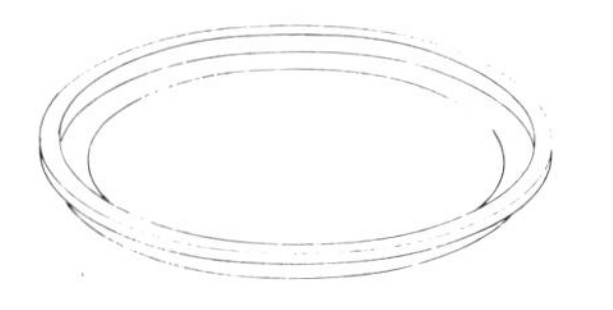
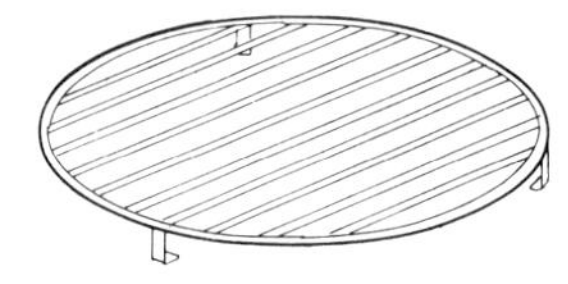
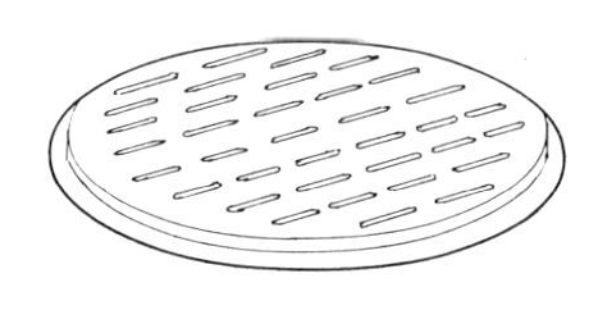
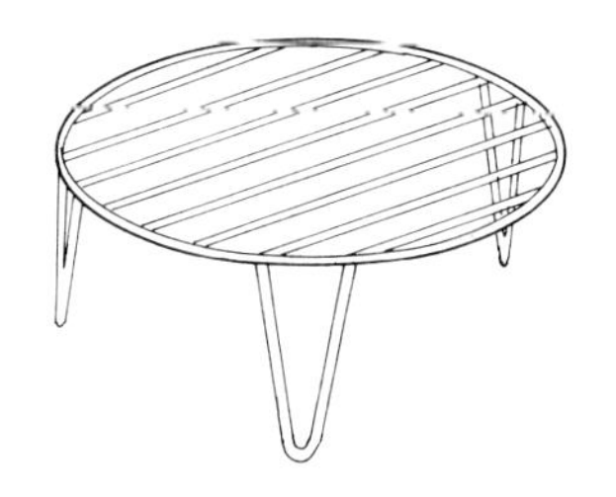

Drip tray and splatter guard

These may be positioned beneath the low rack when roasting joints of meat and poultry during combination or convection cooking. In some models they are used in conjunction with either the high or low rack when grilling or combination grilling. Food may be placed on the rack positioned over the splatter guard or directly on the splatter guard, depending on the thickness of the food and how near it needs to be to the heat source.

Oven shelf

An oven shelf is usually provided if the model does not include a turntable. It is located into runners positioned in the side walls of the oven. Normally there are two or three runner positions to give varying heights for the food, depending on the cooking method being used.

Care and cleaning

Once your combination model has been delivered, it is important to follow the manufacturer's recommendations on siting and installation, even though you may be tempted to begin using it straight away. The instructions will tell you how much gap should be allowed between the cooker and adjacent walls or cabinets, and whether or not it may be positioned near another appliance such as your conventional hob or oven.

Unlike a microwave cooker, the oven cavity in most combination models will get hot during combination and convection cooking. Splatterings from food such as roast meats and grills will be greater than when cooking by microwave alone and will bake onto the interior surfaces. A combination model with halogen heat lamps has the advantage of being easier to clean due to the lack of conventional elements and relatively cooler cavity. A general rule is to clean the oven when it is still warm, preferably after each time it's used, when warm soapy water and a cloth should be sufficient. If splatterings have been allowed to accumulate they may be loosened and softened by the steam from boiling a bowl or jug of water in the oven for about 10 min using microwave only. Harsh abrasives should not be used, but vigorous rubbing will be necessary.

Any removable accessories such as the turntable or racks can be left to soak before cleaning. Remember to wipe the floor of the oven underneath the turntable. Do check the instructions before placing items from the oven into a dishwasher.

Oven sprays should be applied to a cloth before wiping the surfaces. They must never be sprayed directly onto the oven walls as the spray can get in through the vents and cause damage to internal components. Always check with the cooker and oven cleaner manufacturers' instructions before applying any product to make sure that it is suitable for whatever materials your cooker is made of. Incorrectly applied, some cleaners can cause irreversible damage.

After cleaning, rinse thoroughly and dry with a soft cloth. Exterior surfaces can be wiped over with a cloth wrung out in hot soapy water. Touch control panels are best wiped with a water-dampened cloth only. Afterwards buff the surface finishes with a clean dry cloth.

Some manufacturers include catalytic panels on one or two of the oven interior walls which help to burn off splatters as they occur. Manual cleaning of these panels is not usually necessary, but follow any washing or wiping recommendations with care. One or two models include a pyrolitic cleaning cycle. After the oven door is securely locked, the heat in the oven is increased to a temperature where all the splatterings are burned off and reduced to a dust, which is then simply wiped from the compartment.

Suitable utensils

When cooking by the microwave mode alone the general rule is not to use metal tins or dishes, as microwave energy is reflected from metal. How-

A guide to cookware and utensils

Cookware or utensil	Microwave	Convection	Combination	Grill/Combination
Aluminium foil	For shielding	Yes	For shielding	No
Aluminium foil containers	No	Yes	Check oven manufacturer's recommendations	No
Browning dish	Yes	No	No	No
Cooking film	Yes	No	No	No
Disposable paper-board dishes	Yes	Check dish manufacturer's recommendations		No
Freezer to microwave dishes	Yes	No	No	No
Glassware with metal decoration or trims	No	No	No	No
Lead glass	No	No	No	No
Metal tins and cookware	No	Yes	Check oven manufacturer's recommendations	Yes
Oven-to-table ware	If microwave safe	Yes	Yes	Check dish manufacturer's recommendations
Paper	Yes	No	No	No
Plastic microwave cookware	Yes	Check dish manufacturer's recommendations		No
Plastic spatulas	If microwave safe	No	No	No
Precious metal trimmed ovenware	No	Yes	No	No
Pyrex, oven glassware and ceramic	Yes	Yes	Yes	Yes
Roasting bags	Yes	Yes	Yes	No
Thermometers, conventional	No	Yes	No	No
Thermometers, microwave	Yes	No	No	No
Wax paper	Short term heating	No	No	No
Wooden spoons	Yes	No	No	No
Wood, wicker and straw	Yes	No	No	No

ever, this type of cookware is perfectly suitable when cooking with the convection mode, just as metal bakeware is used in conventional cooking. If using your ordinary baking trays, do remember to ensure that they fit and will rotate on the turntable if provided. When it comes to cooking by combination, manufacturers differ in their recommendations with regard to the use of metal cookware, so check with the instructions for your particular model. Experience has shown that the use of metal dishes in combination cooking is inclined to result in certain foods, such as cakes, being overcooked on the top while the base remains relatively pale or even undercooked on occasion. In addition, arcing can sometimes be a problem when a metal tin is placed on a metal turntable or rack. This can be overcome by placing the tin on a suitable heatproof plate so that metal is not in contact with metal. In some models an 'anti-arcing' tray is provided for this purpose.

Plastics on the other hand are extensively used in microwave cooking but to a much lesser degree in convection cooking. Although great improvements have been made with certain plastics in relation to the oven temperatures they are able to withstand, it is unlikely they will be suitable for higher oven temperatures or the direct heat from a grill or halogen heat lamps. Check the container manufacturer's recommendations for maximum oven temperatures before using plastic dishes in convection or combination cooking or grilling.

Remember that the oven cavity, dishes and accessories will become very hot when cooking with either convection, combination or grilling modes, so you will need oven gloves when removing food from the oven. Place the hot dishes onto a heat resistant surface.

Combination temperatures and power levels

Combination convection temperatures and microwave power settings vary slightly between the different manufacturers' models, but cooking is usually carried out at lower microwave power levels to allow food to brown on the surface by convection heat while it is being cooked through by microwave. If high microwave power settings were used, many foods would be overcooked by microwave before they had a chance to brown on the outside.

Convection temperatures recommended by some manufacturers when cooking by combination can be as high as 250°C. This enables very fast browning to take place during microwave cooking. Other manufacturers suggest lower oven temperatures with slightly longer cooking time and experience has shown that this gives a result closer to conventional cooking. Although cooking times are longer with the latter method, it is still possible to save up to 50 per cent over conventional timings – depending on what you are cooking, of course.

The degree and speed of browning is also affected by the construction of the oven and the position of the heat source. For example, combination models with halogen lamps or with forced air convection heating via an element and a fan are inclined to reach temperature more quickly and give slightly faster results (just as conventional fan ovens do) than models with top and bottom heating elements, although these do have the advantage of giving increased top or base browning which can be important for some dishes.

Below are examples of oven temperatures and microwave settings, together with the approximate power (watts) outputs, percentage levels and terminology used at those settings. Do compare these against your own particular model which may vary in output and terminology.

Oven temperatures

The divisions between the temperatures vary slightly between the manufacturers and some may give increases in temperature in 20°C steps.

°Celsius	50....	100....	150....	200....	250
		Cool	Slow	Moderate	Hot	Very hot

Microwave power levels

The actual watts outputs at the different power levels also vary but can be grouped together as shown below:

Watts output Percentage Terminology	65–220 10–36 Low (30%)	254–400 40–60 Medium (50%)	450–500 70–80 Medium/High (70%)	600/650 100 High (100%)

Combination cooking

For the recipes in this book, combination temperatures and microwave power levels are shown as oven temperature followed by microwave terminology with the percentage output in brackets, for example, COMBINATION: 200°C/LOW (30%).

Microwave cooking

Where any cooking is required by microwave alone, this will be given in terminology followed by percentage output in brackets, for example, MICROWAVE: HIGH (100%).

Cooking methods

Combination cooking will produce a wide range of dishes most successfully, but there are some foods which are better cooked by just microwave or just convection. For example, microwave cooking is ideal for fruits, vegetables and fish, and superb casseroles can be achieved by cooking on a low simmer setting. The convection method is preferable for small items of food such as individual pies or tarts, profiteroles, meringues, biscuits, scones and small cakes which are not so successful when cooked by combination, although we have had good results with scone rounds and biscuits which are cut into pieces after cooking.

If you prefer yorkshire puddings which are well risen around the edges and almost flat in the centre then, in our opinion, you will achieve better results by using the convection mode and cooking the pudding in the traditional way. However, good results can be obtained by combination cooking in models which have a **low** but continuous microwave power output, although they are best cooked by convection in cookers with **pulsed** microwave power. We have had no real success with soufflés in combination cookers – they either collapse before you can get them out of the oven, or resemble a pudding mixture rather than a light airy soufflé. Therefore we would recommend that these too should be cooked by convection.

Those cookers which include a grill or grill combination will give better results for foods which are normally grilled, although a similar effect can be achieved on models without this facility by cooking in the combination mode at a high temperature.

Deep fat frying must not be attempted in a combination cooker as the temperature of the fat or oil cannot be controlled. Boiled eggs should be cooked conventionally in a pan of boiling water on the hob. Pancakes too are best cooked in a shallow pan on the hob in the traditional way, although they can be successfully reheated by microwave, or by combination if they are filled.

The table below will help you to choose the cooking method which will produce the best results for whatever you are cooking. On occasions you may need to use more than one cooking method by pre-cooking or preparing food in the microwave and then completing the dish in the combination or convection mode.

Food	Microwave	Convection	Combination	Grill/ Combination
Bacon				*
Beefburgers				*
Biscuits		*		
Bread			*	
Cakes, large			*	
Cakes, small		*		
Casseroles	*		*	
Chicken joints				*
Chops				*
Crumbles			*	
Defrosting	*			
Eggs	*			
Fish	*			
Fruits	*			
Gratinées			*	*
Jacket potatoes			*	
Kebabs				*
Meringues		*		
Pasta	*			
Pastry			*	
Pâtés			*	
Pies, large			*	
Pies, small		*		
Preserves	*			
Profiteroles		*		
Puddings	*			
Pulses	*			
Queen cakes		*		
Quiches			*	
Reheating	*			
Reheating pastry dishes			*	
Roast meat, poultry			*	
Roast potatoes			*	

Food	Micro-wave	Con-vection	Combi-nation	Grill/ Combi-nation
Sauces	*			
Sausages				*
Sausage toad			*	
Scone rounds			*	
Scones		*		
Soufflés		*		
Soups	*			
Sponge cakes		*		
Steaks				*
Surface browning				*
Surface browning and cooking			*	
Vegetables	*			
Yorkshire puddings, (in models with pulsed micro-wave power)		*		
Yorkshire puddings (in models with continuous microwave power)			*	

Success with recipes

Whether you are trying one of the recipes from this book, or attempting some of your own family favourites, here are a few guidelines worthy of consideration before starting to use your combination cooker, to ensure that the very best results are obtained.

Preheating

One of the advantages of combination cooking is that it is not usually necessary to preheat the oven, most cooking being carried out from a cold start. However, one or two manufacturers do recommend a preheat using the convection mode before cooking on combination, particularly when food is placed on two levels. This will ensure that both levels are cooked virtually in the same time, otherwise the contents of one tray may be cooked before the other, or you might have to swop food between the shelves halfway through cooking.

We have also found that cooking from a hot oven or allowing it to preheat can be a distinct advantage for sponge cakes and other light-textured foods which otherwise may be overcooked by microwave before they have browned satisfactorily on the outside. Alternatively, these types of food can be cooked by convection only. In addition, cooking from a hot oven can be an advantage in models with top and bottom elements as they usually take slightly longer to reach temperature than models with fan convection. Combination grilling is carried out from a cold start whereas grilling can be done from either cold or hot – preheating is always required if using the grill to toast bread, teacakes, muffins, scones etc.

For convection cooking, be guided by conventional cooking methods. If you would normally put a dish into a hot oven, then preheat to the required cooking temperature first, remembering to decrease the temperature in the recipe by about 10°C, or as recommended by the cooker manufacturer. Smaller cuts of meat may benefit from being placed in a preheated oven, to obtain maximum browning. The great advantage of combination cookers with halogen lamps as the heat source is that they will not require preheating for either cooking, browning or grilling due to the virtually instant heat output from the lamps.

Breads

Most yeast mixtures cook very well on the combination setting and together with the modern, easy-blend dried yeasts – needing only one proving if you're in a hurry – the hard work is really taken out of bread-making.

After mixing and kneading, the dough should be risen either by leaving in a warm place, or by using the microwave for periods of 15 seconds on HIGH (100%) followed by 5–10 minutes' standing time, repeated until the dough is risen. Shape the dough and place it into a suitable container such as a Pyrex loaf dish. More interesting shapes can be created by using a ceramic dish or by kneading the dough into a round or oval shape and placing it on a heatproof baking plate. Although cooking may take a little longer, by keeping the oven temperature down to 200°C some microwave plastic cookware can be used for combination cooking, but do remember to check with both the dish and cooker manufacturers' instructions.

Depending on the size and shape of the loaf and the type of combination cooker, an oven temperature of 200°C with either a LOW (30%) or MEDIUM (50%) microwave power setting will give you a well risen loaf with a light golden-brown crust. A small loaf will take between 12 and 18 minutes to cook and a large loaf between 18 and 25 minutes. Bread rolls require higher temperatures than loaves in combination cooking in order to brown them quickly during their short cooking time.

You can check whether bread is cooked by tapping the loaf on the base – it should sound slightly hollow. The loaf will probably have browned less on the bottom than when cooking conventionally or by convection only. Some manufacturers may recommend turning the loaf over for the last few minutes of cooking.

Cakes

The cakes which are most successfully cooked on combination are those which are normally cooked at lower temperatures for longer cooking times – rich fruit cakes, gingerbreads, teabreads and madeira cakes for example. These will take between a half and two-thirds less time than when cooked conventionally.

Light sponge cakes can also be cooked by combination, providing the mixture goes into a preheated oven. This will ensure that the cake browns sufficiently during the relatively short cooking time. Alternatively, cook this type of mixture by convection, along with individual biscuits, meringues and small cakes which are not successful when cooked by combination. Preheating may be required when batch baking on two levels to ensure that both levels are cooked in the same time.

Containers such as heatproof glassware or ceramic are ideal for cakes and in addition, cooking at low temperatures means that some microwave plastic cookware will also be suitable, but remember to check with both dish and cooker manufacturers' recommendations. Containers should be lightly greased and the base lined with a circle of baking parchment or greaseproof paper.

Depending on the quantity and type of cake mixture, combination temperatures used range from 160°C to 200°C with LOW (30%) microwave power setting. Cooking will take 10–12 minutes for a light whisked sponge (placed into a preheated oven), and up to about 1 hour for a rich fruit cake. Test the centre of the cake with a skewer to check if it is done – it will come out clean when the cake is cooked through. Leave cakes to stand for 5–10 minutes before removing to a cooling rack, then wrap as soon as possible to prevent them going stale too quickly.

If cooking a cake by convection only, remember to lower the recommended conventional temperature by about 10–20°C and check on its progress before it would normally be ready.

Pastry

Larger pastry dishes such as pies, tarts, quiches and jalousies cook exceptionally well on combination. Small individual pies, jam tarts, mince pies, profiteroles and vol au vents are best cooked by convection heat only. Ceramic dishes are best for quiches and double crust pies as they encourage the base to brown. Alternatively, heatproof glassware may be used. Some manufacturers may provide a baking tray or plate for use in convection and combination cooking, but as metal bakeware prevents microwaves reaching the food, this should not be used on combination unless specifically recommended by a manufacturer.

Pastry flan cases for quiches, flans, bakewell tarts etc should be baked blind by lining with lightly greased greaseproof paper, filling with ceramic baking beans and cooking for 10–15 minutes on combination temperature 200°C with a MEDIUM (50%) microwave setting. Remove the baking beans and paper then leave the pastry case to cool slightly before adding the filling. The combination setting should then be lowered to a temperature of between 160°C and 180°C with a LOW (30%) microwave power setting, and the assembled dish will take a further 15–30 minutes to cook depending on the quantity and type of filling.

Meat pies should have the filling precooked by microwave and then allowed to cool before assembling the dish. Brush pastry with beaten egg for a savoury pie or egg white and caster sugar for a sweet one. The combination temperature should be 200°C with either a LOW (30%) or MEDIUM (50%) microwave power setting depending on the type of pie. With a cooked filling, a single crust pie will take between 20 and 30 minutes to cook and a double crust pie will take 30–40 minutes. Towards the end of cooking, if you feel that the pastry could do with being a little browner, finish off on convection heat only, set to a high temperature, or brown the surface under a preheated grill for a few minutes.

Fish, fruit and vegetables

For fish, fruit and vegetables which are normally poached, boiled or steamed, microwave cooking alone will give the best flavours and tender, moist results. However, if a recipe calls for oven baking when a degree of browning is required – for whole fish; for steaks and cutlets coated in breadcrumbs; for baked whole or stuffed fruit and vegetables; for assembled dishes such as gratinées, crumbles and pies etc – the combination method can be used with very good results.

Prepare the food in the usual way, not forgetting to score or slit the skins of whole fish, fruits and vegetables to prevent them bursting. Brush fish and whole vegetables with a little melted butter or oil and top stuffed vegetables with slivers of butter if required. Cover the food in the dish with a piece of greaseproof paper if you wish, but do not cover with a lid unless the recipe recommends it. Place the dish on the low or recommended rack and cook on combination 180–200°C/LOW (30%) for 10–15 minutes, then check regularly until the food is cooked and lightly golden brown.

Depending on the degree of crispness required for jacket potatoes, these may be cooked at combination setting 200°C/LOW (30%), arranged directly on the baking rack. Alternatively, a 200–250°C/MEDIUM (50%) or HIGH (100%) setting may be used if faster cooking is needed. Potatoes, and other vegetables such as parsnips, required for roasting and serving with a joint can be arranged on the drip tray underneath the meat so that they cook together.

If a little extra browning of a dish is required, increase the combination temperature for the last few minutes of cooking time. Alternatively, finish off under the grill if fitted, or on convection only set to a high temperature for a few minutes at the end of combination cooking.

Meat and poultry

Roasting

For combination cooking, as with microwave cooking, try to choose a joint which is neat and compact in shape. If this is not possible protect thin ends, cut edges and protruding bones with small, smooth pieces of aluminium foil to prevent them from overcooking. It may also be necessary to shield wings and drumsticks of poultry and game birds if over 2kg/4lb in weight. Foil must not be allowed to touch the oven rack or interior walls of the oven or arcing may occur.

Weigh the joint and calculate the cooking time. Brush lean parts with a little melted fat or oil and place fat side up on the low or recommended rack over the drip tray and splatter guard, if fitted. This will ensure that splatterings onto the oven walls and subsequent build up of cooking fumes are kept to a minimum.

Joints of meat over 2kg/4lb with fat on one side should be placed fat side down for the first half of the cooking time. It is good practice to turn all large joints of meat and poultry and game birds to ensure even results, placing poultry breast side down for the first half of cooking. Remember that longer, thinner joints will cook slightly more quickly than joints which are thicker and wider in diameter because the transfer of heat into the centre is faster.

There are no special techniques required when preparing joints of meat and poultry. Prepare as if cooking conventionally; for example, gammon joints should be soaked overnight before cooking, the crackling on pork should be scored, lightly brushed with oil and sprinkled with salt to enhance crispness, and skins of duck and goose should be pricked well with a fork.

The real, traditional roasted flavour is achieved by leaving meat and poultry uncovered during combination cooking, but you may prefer to use a roasting bag to avoid fat splashing in the oven cavity. If you do this, slit it on one side or just tie it loosely to allow steam to escape.

After cooking, cover the joint with a tent of foil (shiny side in) and leave to stand for 10–15 minutes. As with microwave cooking, residual heat will cause the joint to carry on cooking for a short time, and by allowing this rest period the joint will be easier to carve, as with conventional cooking. However, if the meat is cooked to your liking on completion of cooking, it is not essential to let it stand. Juices collected in the drip tray can be used to make the gravy.

Cooking smaller cuts

Small cuts such as chops, sausages, steaks and chicken portions are best cooked by grilling or on grill combination where these features are available, following the manufacturer's recommendations with regard to combination temperatures and settings. Otherwise successful results may be achieved by cooking on convection, or by combination set to a high temperature with LOW (30%) microwave power level.

Weigh the food and calculate the cooking time, brush lean cuts with oil or melted butter, and pierce foods which have a skin, eg sausages and kidneys. Arrange the food directly onto the low or recommended rack positioned over the drip tray with splatter guard where fitted although foods such as kidneys and liver may be placed in a cooking dish if preferred.

The information given in the chart on page 16 is intended as a guide only as the thickness of the meat will affect cooking times. It is advisable to compare these with the recommendations given in the instructions for your particular model before cooking small cuts on combination.

Pot roasts, braising and casseroles

Pot roasts cook well by combination. Weigh the meat and calculate the cooking time. The joint may be braised on a bed of vegetables and some stock or wine added to the dish if desired. Cover with a lid and cook on combination 180–200°C/LOW (30%) allowing about 20–25 minutes per 450g/1lb or until tender, turning the joint if necessary halfway through. For cheaper, tougher joints or cuts for casseroling, cover with stock and reduce to 150–160°C/LOW (30%), allowing 30–45 min per 450g/1lb if required to be cooked on combination, although microwave cooking alone will produce very successful casseroles when cooked on a LOW (30%) power setting.

Combination settings and cooking times for roasts

Manufacturers differ considerably in their recommendations. Suggested combination temperatures can vary between 180°C to 250°C with LOW (30%) or MEDIUM (50%) microwave settings and cooking times vary as much as 10–14 to 19–21 minutes per 450g/1lb for well-done beef. We have found that by keeping to lower temperatures, more traditional results were achieved, with much less splashing and soiling of the oven. However, check with the recommendations given in the instructions for your own model against those given in the chart below and after experimenting for a while, you will be able to determine which method allows you to cook the joint to your taste.

If the calculated cooking time exceeds 50–60 minutes, it may be necessary to reduce the combination temperature by 10–20°C to prevent overbrowning of the outside of the meat. For smaller joints with short cooking times you may find that the joint does not look as brown as you would like it towards the end of cooking, in which case increase the temperature by 10–20°C for the last few minutes, or cook on convection only set to a high temperature for a short time after combination cooking.

A guide to combination settings and cooking times for roast meat and poultry

All meat, poultry and game must be defrosted thoroughly before cooking

Item	Combination temperature and power setting	Cooking time in min per 450g/1lb
Beef		
rare	180°C/LOW (30%)	9–12
medium	180°C/LOW (30%)	12–15
well done	180°C/LOW (30%)	15–18
Chicken	180–200°C/MEDIUM (50%)	10–12
Duck	180–200°C/MEDIUM (50%)	10–12
Game birds	180°C/MEDIUM (50%)	8–10
Gammon	180°C/LOW (30%)	17–20
Goose	180°C/MEDIUM (50%)	10–12
Lamb		
medium	180°C/LOW (30%)	16–19
well done	180°C/LOW (30%)	19–21
Pork	180°C/LOW (30%)	16–20
Pot roasts	180–200°C/LOW (30%)	20–25
Turkey	180°C/MEDIUM (50%)	8–10

A guide to combination settings and cooking times for smaller cuts

More even results will be achieved if all foods are thoroughly defrosted before cooking. In some models a preheat may be required to achieve maximum browning; cooking times may then need to be slightly reduced. Please refer to manufacturer's recommendations when cooking the following items on grill or grill combination if these features are available.

Item	Combination temperature and power setting	Cooking time in min per 450g/1lb
Bacon rashers	250°C/LOW (30%)	8–11
Beefburgers	200°C/LOW (30%)	12–15
Chicken portions	180–200°C/MEDIUM (50%)	14–18
Gammon steaks	200°C/LOW (30%)	13–16
Kidneys	180–200°C/LOW (30%)	14–18
Lamb chops	200–230°C/LOW (30%)	15–19
Liver	180–200°C/LOW (30%)	12–15
Pork chops	200–230°C/LOW (30%)	16–20
Sausages	230°C/LOW (30%)	13–16
Steak		
medium	250°C/LOW (30%)	9–12
well done	230°C/LOW (30%)	15–20
Veal cutlets	200°C/MEDIUM (50%)	13–16

Meal planning

With a little thought and planning, complete meals of two, three or four courses can be cooked in the combination cooker. Experience will help you to become more familiar with cooking and standing times, and many dishes can be prepared in advance then quickly reheated when required without any harm to the food or loss of flavour. Most combination models automatically switch off at the end of the set cooking time so you can leave the next course to heat or cook while eating the first without the worry of food overcooking or spoiling. (Some models, however, only switch off the microwave part of the combination mode, leaving the convection on at the set temperature.)

When first planning your menus, prepare different dishes separately and then gradually progress towards cooking a complete meal. Serve at least one cold course, either a starter or a sweet which can be prepared in advance, and never worry about choosing to serve cold dishes for both of these courses if it saves time when entertaining.

Defrost all foods first, except vegetables which can be cooked from frozen. Foods which require deep-fat frying must be cooked conventionally on a hob as the temperature of the fat or oil cannot be controlled in the combination cooker.

When cooking a joint of meat or poultry on the roasting rack, potatoes and parsnips can be roasted on the splatter guard over the drip tray beneath the joint. The vegetables may be par-boiled by microwave first if preferred. Brush with oil and turn them over halfway through cooking. After removing the meat, it may be necessary to increase the convection temperature by 10–20°C or allow a little longer cooking to brown off the roasted vegetables. Other vegetables are best cooked by microwave, and when large quantities are required, cook them before roasting the meat which then allows more time to make the gravy and reheat sauces.

Yorkshire puddings too should be made during the standing time as they need to be served virtually straight from the oven. Preheat the fat before adding the batter and cook on either combination or convection (see page 12).

You will find it helps to line up the foods in their dishes in the order in which they are to be cooked and, where practicable, for microwaving the vegetables use microwave boiling bags which can be thrown away afterwards. Have aluminium foil ready to 'tent' over the meat during its standing time and to wrap cooked items to keep them warm. If there are a lot of dishes to be served, use the warming compartment or oven at a low setting on a conventional cooker.

Remember to use oven gloves and take care when removing hot dishes and accessories from the combination cooker particularly when cooking on two levels. Place them well onto a heat resistant work surface before dismantling the racks and drip tray. Finally, if a roast meal has been cooked, don't forget to clean the oven while it is still warm!

Combination cooking – reminders and guidelines

- Make sure that you are familiar with the recommendations and advice laid down in the manufacturer's operating instructions.
- Before trying any of the recipes using the temperatures and settings recommended in this book, do refer to the information on page 10 and compare the combination microwave power levels with those on your own particular model as they may vary in output and terminology.
- Always use the accessories as recommended in the cookbook supplied with your model. Most combination cooking is carried out on the low rack or shelf position.
- Get to know any particular characteristics of

your oven and try out the simpler recipes before attempting any more complicated ones.

* Do ensure that you are using the correct cookware and remember that metal bakeware and containers will prevent microwaves from reaching the food (see page 9).
* Base browning is increased by the use of dark or non-stick metal bakeware (usually recommended on convection mode only), otherwise in some models, it may be necessary to turn foods such as bread and biscuits over during cooking.
* Check that you are using the best cooking method for the various food categories (see pages 11/12).
* Most combination cooking is carried out from a cold start, but do check with the manufacturer's operating instructions about preheating in your particular model (see page 12).
* Remember that if your combination cooker includes fan convection, it will reach temperature and brown more quickly than models with top and base elements only. Recipes in this book have been developed for cooking on fan convection models although some have also been tested on models with top and bottom elements. Extra cooking time may need to be allowed if using this type of combination cooker.
* If at the end of combination cooking, foods such as bread or roast meat, poultry or potatoes, are not sufficiently browned for your liking, finish off on convection only set to a high temperature for a few minutes.
* When cooking by convection only, follow your own conventional recipes but reduce the temperature by about 10°C or as the manufacturer recommends, and be prepared to check the food before it would normally be ready.
* Combination cookers with halogen lamps as the heat source for browning do not require an oven temperature to be set. When trying recipes from this book, compare them with a similar one from the manufacturer's cookbook and be guided by the recommended cooking method and timings.
* If necessary, faster browning may be achieved on some combination cookers by increasing the temperatures recommended in this book by 20–30°C but be guided by the manufacturer's temperature recommendations for your model.
* After cooking baked products – bread and cakes for example – wrap, decorate or ice them as soon as possible to avoid them becoming stale too quickly through excess moisture loss.
* If in doubt about which combination setting to use, a temperature of 180–200°C with a LOW (30%) microwave power setting will cook most savoury foods. Give a minimum time of 10 minutes cooking and then check every 3 minutes until cooked.
* The recipes in this book have been tested on a wide range of models, but remember that the actual length of combination cooking times in your particular model depends on both the convection oven temperature and the microwave power output at any given setting. These vary between cookers, not only due to the differences in design but also due to the tolerances on oven thermostats, magnetrons and controls. Therefore, slight adjustment to the convection temperatures and microwave power levels or cooking times may be required to ensure best results.

Above: Curried Choux Crown (page 20)
below: Spiced Red Mullet with Banana (page 25); right: Baked Snails (page 20)

Appetisers and starters

Appetisers and starters

Baked snails

(serves 2–3) colour page 19

MICROWAVE: MEDIUM (50%)
COMBINATION: 180°C/LOW (30%)

25g/1oz butter
1 clove garlic, crushed
200g/7oz can snails, drained
1×15ml/tbsp brandy
1×15ml/tbsp chopped parsley
salt and pepper
2×15ml/tbsp double cream

for garnish: freshly chopped parsley

1 Heat the butter in a suitable casserole dish for 30–60 sec. Add the garlic and the snails and cook, covered, for 5 min on the low rack on combination 180°C/LOW.
2 Remove the casserole from the oven. Place the brandy in a cup or saucer and heat for 20 sec on microwave HIGH. Remove from the oven and ignite the brandy, then pour over the snails.
3 Add the chopped parsley to the snails and season to taste with salt and pepper. Stir in the cream. Heat for 2–3 min on microwave MEDIUM, if necessary.
4 Serve the snails, garnished with a little extra parsley, with triangles of toast.

Cook's note: *Canned snails are available in good delicatessens. Choose the large snails. Most canned snails come from France or China*

Curried choux crown

(serves 6–8) colour page 18

MICROWAVE: HIGH (100%)
COMBINATION: 200°C/LOW (30%)

for the choux pastry:
50g/2oz butter or margarine
150ml/5fl oz water
8×15ml/tbsp plain flour, sieved
2 eggs, beaten
oil

for the curried chicken sauce:
2×15ml/tbsp oil
1 onion, chopped
1 clove garlic, crushed
1×15ml/tsp curry powder
375g/12oz boneless chicken breasts, finely diced
400g/14oz can tomatoes
2×15ml/tbsp tomato purée

for the yogurt sauce:
1 large bunch coriander leaves
1 lemon, grated rind
150ml/5fl oz set natural yogurt

1 Prepare the choux pastry. Place the butter or margarine and water in a bowl and heat for 4–5 min on microwave HIGH until boiling rapidly.
2 Place the sieved flour on a saucer. Shoot the flour into the butter and water as soon as you open the microwave door – the mixture must be boiling rapidly in order for it to absorb the flour grains and thicken. Beat the mixture until it forms a ball, leaving the sides of the dish. Allow to cool slightly.
3 Gradually beat the eggs into the pastry to give a smooth, glossy dough of piping consistency.
4 Lightly oil a 20cm/8in round glass dish. Arrange the pastry in twelve spoonfuls around the edge of the dish, leaving the centre of the dish empty.
5 Preheat the oven for 10 min on convection 200°C. Place the choux ring in the hot oven and cook for 20 min on the low rack on combination 200°C/LOW. Slit the choux pastry in several places and continue to cook for a further 5–8 min, until crisp and well browned.
6 Remove the choux ring to a cooling rack immediately and allow to cool completely.
7 Heat the oil in a suitable casserole dish for 2 min on microwave HIGH. Add the onion, garlic and curry powder and cook, covered, for 3 min.
8 Add the chicken to the dish and cook for a further 4 min, covered, stirring once during cooking. Add the tomatoes and tomato purée and cook, uncovered, for 15 min, until thick. Allow to cool completely.

9 Spoon the cold chicken mixture over the choux pastry.
10 Finely chop most of the coriander. Beat the lemon rind and chopped coriander into the yogurt. Pour the yogurt over the top of the chicken sauce and garnish with the remaining coriander leaves.
11 Serve chilled, with a little shredded lettuce.

Salmon pots

(serves 4)

COMBINATION: 160°C/LOW (30%)

This is an economical way of creating a dish of sheer luxury, using both fresh and smoked salmon

butter
125g/4oz smoked salmon
1 salmon tail, weighing approx 225g/8oz
salt and white pepper
lemon juice
125ml/4fl oz single cream
1 egg, beaten
chopped chives

for serving: avocado, mayonnaise and brown bread and butter

1 Lightly butter 4 ramekin dishes and line the sides and bases with smoked salmon. Use either slices or large, thin pieces.
2 Skin the salmon tail with a sharp knife. Cut the flesh from the bone in 4 fillets by cutting down the bone on one side, removing 2 fillets, then repeating on the other side of the tail.
3 Season the fillets lightly with salt and pepper then sprinkle with a few drops of lemon juice. Roll the fillets and put one in each ramekin, placing the end of the roll on the base of each lined dish.
4 Beat together the cream and the egg and add salt and pepper and a few chopped chives. Pour the custard into the ramekins.
5 Cook on the low rack on combination 160°C/LOW for 10 min, until the custard is just set and the salmon is tender when tested with a sharp knife or a skewer.
6 Allow to cool then chill in the refrigerator for 2 hr.
7 Loosen the fish from the edges of the dishes and invert onto serving plates. Garnish with a salad of sliced avocado in lemon juice and a little extra smoked salmon. Serve with mayonnaise and brown bread and butter.

Pork and ginger terrine with apricot sauce

(serves 8)

COMBINATION: 160°C/LOW (30%)

Pork, ginger and apricot make a wonderful combination of flavours. Pâtés and terrines are very popular starters, but this one is unusual, in that it is served with a fruit sauce

8 rashers streaky bacon, rinded
350g/12oz belly pork rashers, rinded
225g/8oz pigs liver
1 small onion
50g/2oz crystalised ginger
salt and pepper
1×15ml/tbsp brandy
400g/14oz can apricots in natural juice
2×15ml/tbsp freshly chopped coriander leaves or rosemary
1 egg, beaten

for garnish: fresh coriander or rosemary

1 Lightly grease a 450g/1lb ovenproof glass loaf dish and line with the bacon.
2 Coarsely mince the belly pork, liver, onion and half the ginger. Season the mixture with salt and pepper, then add the brandy and 2×15ml/tbsp juice from the apricots.
3 Finally add half the coriander or rosemary to the pâté mixture with the beaten egg and mix well.
4 Turn the pâté into the prepared loaf dish and cook on the low rack on combination 160°C/LOW for 20 min.
5 Press the terrine under a heavy weight and chill for 6–8 hr. Loosen the terrine from the sides of the dish with a palette knife and turn out onto a plate.
6 Prepare a sauce by liquidising the apricots and the remaining juice with the rest of the ginger and coriander or rosemary. Add a little pepper to taste.
7 Serve the terrine on individual plates. Flood each plate with a little of the sauce and place a slice of terrine in the centre. Garnish with a little coriander or rosemary and serve with a roll or toast.

Cook's note: *Don't try to carry servings on a bed of sauce very far – a tide-mark caused by a shaky hand looks very untidy! Serve the terrine on a surface close to the dining table*

Prawns in parsley butter

(serves 4) colour opposite

COMBINATION: 200°C/LOW (30%)

Crushed garlic goes wonderfully with this simple prawn starter, but do remember that not everyone likes this traditional French flavouring. If the garlic is omitted, the parsley gives a very delicate flavour to the prawns

450g/1lb prawns
50g/2oz butter
2×15ml/tbsp freshly chopped parsley
1–2 cloves garlic, crushed (optional)
salt and pepper
lemon juice

1 Place the prawns in an ovenproof dish and dot with the butter. Sprinkle with the parsley, garlic (if used) and a little salt and pepper.
2 Cook, uncovered, on the low rack on combination 200°C/LOW for 10 min.
3 Sprinkle with a few drops of lemon juice and serve immediately, with bread.

Roquefort stuffed mushrooms

(serves 4) colour opposite

MICROWAVE: HIGH (100%)
COMBINATION: 200°C/LOW (30%)

4 large cup mushrooms, weighing about 50g/2oz each
50g/2oz butter or margarine
1 onion, finely chopped
1 clove garlic, crushed
50g/2oz brown breadcrumbs
1×15ml/tbsp freshly chopped chives
salt and pepper
125g/4oz roquefort cheese, crumbled

for garnish: parsley and tomato slices

1 Peel the mushrooms and place them in a serving dish. Cut off the stalks and chop finely.
2 Melt the butter or margarine in a dish for 1–2 min on microwave HIGH, add the onion, garlic and any chopped mushroom stalks. Cover and cook for 2 min.
3 Stir the breadcrumbs and chives into the onions, then season with salt and pepper. Finally, add the crumbled roquefort cheese.
4 Pile the filling into the four mushrooms. Cook on the low rack on combination 200°C/LOW for 8–10 min.
5 Serve, garnished with parsley and tomato slices, with warm toast.

Baked camembert

(serves 4) colour opposite

COMBINATION: 200°C/LOW (30%)

Baked camembert makes a rich starter, ideal before a plain main course. Use either one whole camembert, or 4 small portions, completely enclosed in a skin

1×250g/9oz camembert, or 4 small portions

for serving: 4×5ml/tsp cranberry sauce or blackcurrant jam and toast or melba toast

1 Preheat the oven for 10 min on convection 200°C.
2 Place the camembert on an ovenproof plate and heat for 5 min on the low rack on combination 200°C/LOW.
3 If using a large camembert, cut carefully and place on individual serving plates. Serve with cranberry sauce or blackcurrant jam, and toast or melba toast.

Pâté maison pie

(serves 8)

MICROWAVE: HIGH (100%)
COMBINATION: 180°C/MEDIUM (50%) and 200°C/MEDIUM (50%)

The traditional pâté maison, made with chicken livers and plenty of butter, is very rich. By cutting down on the butter and serving the pâté in a pastry shell you create a starter which will not spoil your appetite for the following courses

for the pastry:
175g/6oz flour
pinch salt
75g/3oz butter or margarine
water to mix

for the pâté:
450g/1lb chicken livers
175g/6oz butter
2×15ml/tbsp brandy
salt and black pepper
3 bay leaves

1 Prepare the pastry by placing the flour and salt in a bowl and rubbing in the butter or margarine until the mixture resembles fine breadcrumbs. Add sufficient cold water to form

Prawns in Parsley Butter (above); Roquefort Stuffed Mushrooms (above); Baked Camembert (above)

a stiff dough, then roll out and use to line a suitable shallow 20cm/8in round flan dish.

2 Prick the base of the pastry then line with greaseproof paper and bake blind, on the low rack, for 10 min on combination 200°C/MEDIUM.

3 Prepare the pâté. Place the chicken livers in a suitable casserole with 125g/4oz of the butter, cut into pieces. Heat the brandy for 20 sec on microwave HIGH then remove from the cooker and ignite. Pour the brandy over the livers. Cover and cook for 10 min on the low rack on combination 180°C/MEDIUM.

4 Liquidise the pâté in a blender or processor until smooth, then season to taste with salt and pepper. Spoon the pâté into the pastry shell.

5 Heat the remaining butter on microwave HIGH for 1–1½ min, until melted. Arrange the bay leaves on the pâté then pour the melted butter over. Leave to cool then chill for 1–2 hr before serving with salad.

Mussels with white wine and brandy

(serves 4)

MICROWAVE: HIGH (100%)
COMBINATION: 180°C/MEDIUM (50%)

1 small onion, finely sliced
900g/2lb mussels, washed
1 bay leaf
150ml/5fl oz dry white wine
150ml/5fl oz single or soured cream
salt and pepper

for garnish: freshly chopped parsley
for dunking: french bread

1 Cook the onion in a large suitable casserole dish for 2 min, covered, on microwave HIGH. Add the mussels, bay leaf and wine and cook for a further 5 min, covered, until all the mussels have opened.

2 Allow the mussels to cool slightly then remove one shell from each. Remove the bay leaf from the dish. Stir the cream into the stock with some salt and pepper then return the mussels to the dish.

3 Cook on the low rack on combination 180°C/MEDIUM for 10 min, until piping hot.

4 Sprinkle with chopped parsley then serve immediately. Use fresh french bread to savour the final delights of the sauce.

Scallops with asparagus

(serves 3–4) *colour page 75*

MICROWAVE: HIGH (100%)
COMBINATION: 180°C/LOW (30%) and 200°C/MEDIUM (50%)

Prepare this delicious dish for a special occasion in the spring, when both scallops and asparagus are fresh and plentiful

6 thin spears fresh asparagus
275ml/10fl oz milk, approx
2×15ml/tbsp white wine
6 very large scallops, cleaned
25g/1oz butter or margarine
25g/1oz flour
3×15ml/tbsp double cream
salt and white pepper
40–50g/1½–2oz gruyère cheese, grated

1 Trim the asparagus and cut the tips to a length of 7.5cm/3in. Finely slice the remainder of the spears. Place in a bowl with 150ml/5fl oz of the milk and the white wine, cover and cook for 5–6 min on microwave HIGH, until just tender.

2 Remove the asparagus and reserve. Skim the cooking liquor, removing any sediment or scum.

3 Add the scallops to the cooking liquor, cover and cook for 8–10 min on the low rack on combination 180°C/LOW. The scallops should offer no resistance when tested with a skewer. Remove the scallops from the cooking liquor and slice horizontally.

4 Heat the cooking juices for 4–5 min on microwave HIGH, until well reduced. Strain the liquor and reserve.

5 Heat the butter or margarine in a bowl on microwave HIGH for 1–2 min. Stir in the flour.

6 Add sufficient milk to the cooking juices to give 200ml/7fl oz. Gradually add the liquid to the butter and flour then heat for 3–4 min on microwave HIGH, until boiling and thickened.

7 Add the cream to the sauce then season to taste with salt and white pepper.

8 Carefully combine the scallops and chopped asparagus in the sauce then turn into a serving dish. Sprinkle with the grated gruyère cheese.

9 Heat for 5–6 min on combination 200°C/MEDIUM until warmed through, and the cheese is melted. For extra browning, cook for 2–3 min on grill combination, or under a conventional, preheated grill. Serve immediately.

Spiced red mullet with banana

(serves 4) colour page 18

MICROWAVE: HIGH (100%)
COMBINATION: 200°C/LOW (30%)

4 red mullet, weighing about 150–175g/5–6oz each
2×15ml/tbsp oil
1 small onion, finely sliced
½ green chilli, finely chopped
1×5ml/tsp ground ginger
salt and pepper
150ml/5fl oz boiling fish or vegetable stock
2 bananas, sliced
fresh lemon juice

for serving: lettuce or spinach and natural set yogurt

1 Clean and descale the fish.
2 Heat the oil in a shallow serving dish for 2 min on microwave HIGH, add the onion, chilli and ground ginger and cook for 3 min, covered.
3 Add the fish, season with salt and pepper then pour the stock over.
4 Cover the dish and cook on the low rack on combination 200°C/LOW for 10 min.
5 Add the banana and lemon juice to the dish and cook, uncovered, for a further 5 min.
6 Serve each fish on a bed of shredded lettuce or fresh raw spinach, with a little of the juice and some set natural yogurt.

Cook's note: *Red mullet should really be cleaned and cooked with only the liver inside the fish. As they are quite small fish, however, they are often cooked without being cleaned*

Crab and avocado cheesecake

(serves 8) colour page 79

COMBINATION: 200°C/MEDIUM (50%) and 160°C/LOW (30%)

125g/4oz plain flour
salt
paprika
50g/2oz butter or margarine
water to mix

for the filling
400g/14oz cream cheese
3 eggs, separated
1 lemon, grated rind and juice
25g/1oz flour
1 ripe avocado, peeled and chopped
170g/6oz can white crab meat, drained
few drops tabasco sauce (optional)

for garnish: sliced avocado
for serving: tomato salad

1 Prepare the pastry by placing the flour, salt and paprika in a bowl and rubbing in the butter or margarine until the mixture resembles fine breadcrumbs. Add sufficient cold water to form a stiff dough. Knead the pastry gently on a floured surface then roll out and use to line a 20cm/8in ovenproof glass flan dish. Prick the base of the pastry with a fork.
2 Bake the pastry shell blind for 10 min on the low rack on combination 200°C/MEDIUM.
3 Beat the cream cheese until smooth then add the egg yolks, lemon rind and juice, a good pinch each of salt and paprika and the flour. Beat well until smooth. Add the avocado, crab meat and tabasco, if used, and beat well.
4 Whisk the egg whites until stiff then fold into the avocado mixture. Spoon the mixture into the pastry shell and smooth the top.
5 Cook on the low rack on combination 160°C/LOW for 30 min until browned and set. Allow to cool.
6 Decorate with avocado slices and serve with a small tomato salad.

Brunches, snacks and suppers

Above: Bacon and Mussel Pasta (page 28)
left: Gazpacho Tart (page 28)
right: Sandwich Supper Pudding (page 28)

Brunches, snacks and suppers

Gazpacho tart

(serves 8) colour page 26

MICROWAVE: HIGH (100%)
COMBINATION: 200°C/MEDIUM (50%)

This unusual vegetable tart makes a good supper dish when served with a small side salad

125g/4oz fresh brown breadcrumbs
125g/4oz mixed nuts, finely chopped
1×15ml/tbsp freshly chopped mint
salt and pepper
3 egg whites
425ml/15fl oz boiling water
1×pkt aspic powder
2×15ml/tbsp tomato purée
½ red pepper, finely chopped
½ green pepper, finely chopped
¼ cucumber, finely diced
1 clove garlic, crushed

for garnish: pepper rings

1 Lightly grease a 20cm/8in round flan dish. If the dish does not have a removable base, line the bottom with baking parchment.
2 Place the breadcrumbs, nuts, mint and seasonings in a bowl. Whisk the egg whites until stiff then fold them into the breadcrumb mixture. Spoon the mixture into the prepared dish and smooth the surface with a metal spoon.
3 Cook on the low rack on combination 200°C/MEDIUM for 15 min, until firm and golden brown. If the dish does not have a removable base, loosen the crust from the sides of the dish before leaving to cool.
4 Pour the boiling water into a jug and add the aspic. Stir well and heat for 15 sec on microwave HIGH to completely dissolve the powder. Stir in the tomato purée and leave to cool.
5 Toss the diced peppers, cucumber and garlic in the cooled aspic then spoon them into the dish on top of the breadcrumb and nut base. Pour the tomato aspic over the vegetables then refrigerate until set.
6 Garnish with pepper rings before serving with a side salad.

Sandwich supper pudding

(serves 4) colour page 27

COMBINATION: 180°C/LOW (30%)

8 slices bread, crusts removed
butter or margarine for spreading
375g/12oz can asparagus, drained
125g/4oz sliced ham
425ml/15fl oz milk
3 eggs, beaten
salt and pepper
75g/3oz cheddar cheese, grated

for garnish: asparagus or tomato slices

1 Spread the bread with butter or margarine. Prepare four sandwiches, filled with the drained asparagus and sliced ham, and having the buttered side of the bread on the outside of the sandwiches.
2 Cut the sandwiches into triangles and arrange them in a 20cm/8in round shallow dish.
3 Beat the milk, eggs and salt and pepper together and pour over the sandwiches. Allow to stand for 20 min.
4 Scatter the cheese over the dish and cook on the low rack on combination 180°C/LOW for 10 min, until the cheese has melted and browned and the pudding is set.
5 Garnish with asparagus or tomato slices and serve immediately.

Bacon and mussel pasta

(serves 3–4) colour page 26

MICROWAVE: HIGH (100%)
COMBINATION: 200°C/MEDIUM (50%)

225g/8oz pasta spirals
1×15ml/tbsp oil
salt
225g/8oz bacon pieces, trimmed
2 cloves garlic, crushed
150ml/5fl oz soured cream
150ml/5fl oz natural yogurt
225g/8oz can mussels, drained
pepper

for garnish: freshly chopped parsley

1. Bring a large pan of water to the boil on the hob. Add the oil and a pinch of salt and the pasta and boil as directed on the packet.
2. Place the bacon and the garlic in a covered casserole dish and cook for 6 min on microwave HIGH, stirring once.
3. Drain the pasta and add it to the bacon. Combine the soured cream and yogurt and pour over the pasta. Add the mussels, salt and pepper and toss the ingredients together.
4. Heat, uncovered, for 10 min on the low rack on combination 200°C/MEDIUM. Some of the pasta will become crispy during heating.
5. Garnish with chopped parsley and serve with a side salad.

Cook's note: *The pasta may be cooked in plenty of boiling water, covered, on microwave HIGH for 6–8 min*

Bacon and egg fiesta

(serves 3)

COMBINATION: 200°C/MEDIUM (50%) and 200°C/LOW (30%)

An ideal brunch or supper dish

6 slices medium cut white bread
butter or margarine for spreading
5 eggs
salt and pepper
6 rashers thinly sliced back bacon
3 tomatoes, sliced
paprika pepper

1. Cut the crusts from the bread and cut the slices into halves diagonally. Spread each piece of bread with butter or margarine.
2. Beat two of the eggs in a small bowl with a pinch of salt and a little pepper. Dip the pieces of bread in the beaten egg then arrange them in a suitable shallow 20cm/8in round flan dish. Pour any remaining egg over the bread.
3. Lay the bacon rashers over the bread then top with the sliced tomatoes. Cook on the low rack on combination 200°C/MEDIUM for 10 min.
4. Break the remaining eggs into the dish over the tomatoes. Prick the yolks and continue to cook for a further 4–5 min on combination 200°C/LOW. Sprinkle with paprika pepper then serve immediately.

Moussaka

(serves 4)

MICROWAVE: HIGH (100%)
COMBINATION: 200°C/MEDIUM (50%)

The combination of oregano and cinnamon give this traditional Greek dish the flavour of the Mediterranean

2×15ml/tbsp olive oil
2 medium aubergines, sliced
1 large onion, chopped
1 clove garlic, crushed
450g/1lb minced lamb
400g/14oz can chopped tomatoes
1×15ml/tbsp tomato purée
salt and pepper
1×5ml/tsp dried oregano or mixed herbs
25g/1oz butter or margarine
25g/1oz flour
150ml/5fl oz milk
150ml/5fl oz soured cream
pinch cinnamon
125g/4oz feta cheese, crumbled

for serving: salad

1. Place the oil and aubergines in a suitable casserole dish. Cover and cook for 10 min on microwave HIGH. Stir once during cooking. Remove the aubergine slices and reserve.
2. Add the onion and garlic to the juices in the casserole and cook, covered, for 2 min. Add the minced lamb and cook for a further 4 min, covered. Stir once during cooking.
3. Add the canned tomatoes, tomato purée, salt and pepper and dried oregano or herbs. Cook, uncovered, for 10 min on microwave HIGH.
4. Remove half the mince from the dish. Layer half the aubergine over the remaining meat then repeat the layers with the remaining ingredients.
5. Prepare a sauce by heating the butter or margarine on microwave HIGH for 1 min. Stir in the flour then gradually add the milk. Heat for 2 min, stirring several times, until very thick.
6. Whisk the soured cream into the sauce with the cinnamon, then add half the feta cheese. Season to taste then spoon into the casserole over the aubergines. Scatter the remaining feta over the top.
7. Cook on the low rack on combination 200°C/MEDIUM for 20 min until piping hot and browned.
8. Serve immediately with salad.

Chicken and ginger tacos

(serves 3) colour opposite

MICROWAVE: HIGH (100%)
COMBINATION: 180°C/LOW (30%) and 200°C/MEDIUM (50%)

Tacos are the easiest of Mexican foods to prepare. This chicken and ginger filling makes a good alternative to the traditional minced beef

25g/1oz butter or margarine
25g/1oz almonds, chopped
1 clove garlic, crushed
350g/12oz boneless chicken breasts, finely chopped
35g/1.25oz packet taco seasoning mix
175g/6fl oz hot water
25g/1oz crystallised ginger
1×15ml/tbsp freshly chopped coriander
6 taco shells
1 avocado
lemon juice

for serving: shredded lettuce, chopped tomato, grated cheese, olives and taco sauce

1. Melt the butter in a suitable casserole dish for 1–2 min on microwave HIGH. Add the almonds and garlic and cook for 2 min, until the almonds are browned.
2. Toss the chicken in the taco seasoning, then stir the chicken and seasoning into the almonds and cook, covered, for 4 min, stirring once during cooking.
3. Add the hot water to the casserole with the crystallised ginger and the coriander. Cover the dish and cook on the low rack on combination 180°C/LOW for 15 min.
4. Remove the lid from the casserole and cook the filling for 5 min on microwave HIGH to reduce and thicken the sauce. Cover the dish and set aside.
5. Place the taco shells on their open sides on a suitable plate or shallow dish. Heat for 3–4 min on the low rack on combination 200°C/MEDIUM.
6. While the tacos are heating, peel and chop the avocado and toss in lemon juice. Stir into the chicken filling.
7. Place a little of the chicken in the base of each taco shell, then top with shredded lettuce, chopped tomatoes, grated cheese, olives and taco sauce before serving.

Cook's note: *Always heat taco shells on their open end, otherwise the shell will collapse and be impossible to fill.*

Tuna scone pizza

(serves 4–6) colour opposite

MICROWAVE: HIGH (100%)
COMBINATION: 200°C/LOW (30%)

This pizza is made with a scone base, which is quick and easy both to prepare and to cook

for the sauce:
2×15ml/tbsp oil
1 onion, finely chopped
1 clove garlic, crushed
½ red pepper, finely chopped
200g/7oz can tuna fish, drained
salt and pepper
1×15ml/tbsp freshly chopped oregano
400g/14oz can chopped tomatoes
1×15ml/tbsp tomato purée

for the scone base:
125g/4oz self-raising flour
pinch each salt and dry mustard
40g/1½oz butter or margarine
50g/2oz cheddar cheese, grated
milk to mix

for the topping:
50g/2oz cheddar cheese, grated
50g/2oz can anchovy fillets, drained and soaked in milk
olives

1. Place the oil, onion and garlic in a large dish, cover and cook for 2 min on microwave HIGH. Add all the remaining ingredients for the sauce and cook for 10–12 min, uncovered, until reduced and thickened. Season to taste.
2. While the sauce is cooking prepare the scone base. Place the flour, salt and mustard powder in a bowl and rub in the butter or margarine. Stir in the grated cheese then add sufficient milk to form a soft scone dough.
3. Lightly knead the dough on a floured surface and roll out to line a 22.5cm/10in ovenproof glass plate or pizza dish.
4. Spoon the sauce over the scone dough and top with the grated cheese. Arrange the drained anchovies and olives on the cheese.
5. Cook for 15–18 min on the low rack on combination 200°C/LOW, until the base is cooked and the cheese is melted and browned.
6. Serve immediately with a side salad.

Tuna Scone Pizza (above); Chicken and Ginger Tacos (above)

Fish and Potato Pie

(serves 4)

MICROWAVE: HIGH (100%)
COMBINATION: 200°C/MEDIUM (50%)

575g/1¼lb potatoes, peeled
40g/1½oz butter or margarine
125g/4oz mushrooms, sliced
40g/1½oz flour
425ml/15fl oz milk
1×15ml/tbsp freshly chopped parsley (optional)
salt and pepper
675g/1½lb white fish, cod, haddock, coley, etc
butter
milk

1. Cut the potatoes into small pieces. Bring to the boil in a pan of water on the hob, then simmer until cooked. Drain.
2. While the potatoes are cooking, prepare the sauce. Heat the butter or margarine in a bowl or jug for 1 min on microwave HIGH. Add the mushrooms and cook, covered, for 3 min. Stir in the flour then gradually add the milk. Heat for 4–5 min on microwave HIGH, stirring every minute, until boiling and thickened.
3. Add the parsley to the sauce with salt and pepper to taste.
4. Arrange the fish in the bottom of a suitable casserole dish and pour the sauce over.
5. Mash the potatoes, adding a little butter and milk. Pile the potato into the dish and smooth the surface with a fork.
6. Cook on the low rack on combination 200°C/MEDIUM for 15–18 min. Serve with freshly cooked vegetables or a mixed salad.

Sausage and bacon plait

(serves 4)

MICROWAVE: HIGH (100%)
COMBINATION: 200°C/MEDIUM (50%)

1 onion, finely chopped
2 stalks celery, finely chopped
225g/8oz prepared puff pastry
3 rashers back bacon
450g/1lb sausagemeat
1×15ml/tbsp tomato purée
salt and pepper
1×5ml/tsp dried mixed herbs
1 egg, beaten

1. Place the onion and celery in a covered microwave dish and cook on microwave HIGH for 4 min, stirring once during cooking. Allow to cool slightly.
2. Roll out the pastry into a large rectangle, measuring approx 20×30.5cm/8×12in. Lay the bacon across the pastry.
3. Beat the sausagemeat into the onion and celery with the tomato purée, seasoning and herbs. Pile the mixture down the middle of the pastry.
4. Brush the pastry with beaten egg then cut the pastry to each side of the sausagemeat into an equal number of strips.
5. Fold the pastry at each end over the sausagemeat then overlap the pastry strips over the filling to form a plait.
6. Place the plait on a suitable baking dish or ovenproof plate and brush with beaten egg.
7. Cook on the low rack on combination 200°C/MEDIUM for 18–20 min, until the pastry is puffed and golden brown.
8. Serve hot or cold with salad.

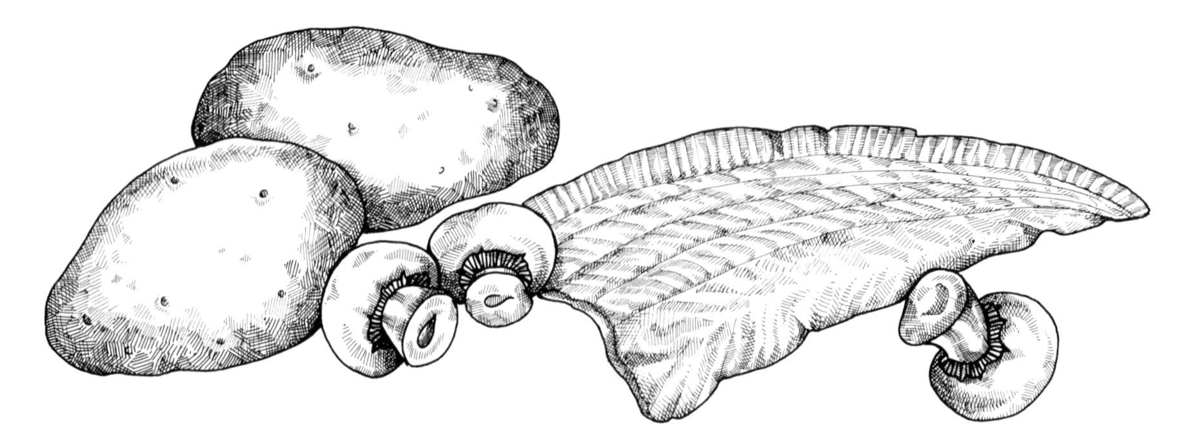

Tortilla chip pie

(serves 4)

MICROWAVE: HIGH (100%)
COMBINATION: 200°C/MEDIUM (50%) and 200°C/LOW (30%)

Mexicans serve a traditional taco pie using crushed taco shells. Tortilla chip pie has the true flavour of Mexico

for the pastry:
175g/6oz flour
pinch salt
75g/3oz butter or margarine
water to mix

for the filling:
450g/1lb minced beef
35g/1.25oz packet taco seasoning mix
water
1 ripe avocado, peeled and chopped
juice of half lemon
3×15ml/tbsp soured cream
chilli sauce to taste
2 tomatoes, chopped
2–3×15ml/tbsp olives
50g/2oz cheddar cheese, grated
tortilla chips, roughly crushed (about a handful)
1 shredded lettuce

1. Prepare the pastry by placing the flour and salt in a bowl and rubbing in the butter or margarine until the mixture resembles fine breadcrumbs. Add sufficient cold water to make a stiff dough, then roll out the pastry and use to line a 20cm/8in round flan dish. Prick the base and bake blind for 10 min on the low rack on combination 200°C/MEDIUM.
2. Place the minced beef in a covered casserole with the taco seasoning mix. Cover and cook for 4 min on microwave HIGH, stirring once. Add water, as directed on the seasoning packet, and cook, uncovered, for 12–15 min, until reduced and thickened.
3. Spoon the minced beef into the pastry case and smooth the top.
4. Place the avocado in a liquidiser or food processor with the lemon juice, soured cream and chilli sauce. Liquidise to a smooth purée then spoon over the minced beef.
5. Top the avocado with the chopped tomatoes and olives then sprinkle with the grated cheese.
6. Cook on the low rack on combination 200°C/LOW for 15 min, until the cheese is melted and browned.
7. Top the pie with crushed tortilla chips and shredded lettuce, and serve hot.

Kipper and leek cream bake

(serves 3–4)

MICROWAVE: HIGH (100%)
COMBINATION: 200°C/LOW (30%)

350g/12oz kipper fillets
25g/1oz butter or margarine
225g/8oz leeks, trimmed, washed and sliced
black pepper
150ml/5fl oz single cream
40g/1½oz fresh breadcrumbs

1. Place the kipper fillets in a 20cm/8in shallow dish and dot with the butter. Cover and cook for 5 min on microwave HIGH.
2. Remove the kippers from the dish and allow to cool slightly before skinning.
3. Place the leeks in the dish and cook in the juices for 4 min, covered, stirring once during cooking.
4. Skin the kipper fillets and keep the flesh in large pieces. Return the kippers to the dish with the leeks and carefully stir in a little black pepper and the cream. Scatter the breadcrumbs over the dish.
5. Cook for 10 min on the low rack on combination 200°C/LOW.
6. Serve immediately with a tomato salad.

Crispy chicken drumsticks

(serves 4)

COMBINATION: 200°C/MEDIUM (50%)

These drumsticks are delicious hot or cold

8 chicken drumsticks (total weight approx 775g/1¾lb)
75g/3oz dried breadcrumbs, wholewheat or golden
50g/2oz cheddar cheese, grated
1 clove garlic, crushed
1×5ml/tsp paprika pepper
pinch salt
1 egg, beaten

1. Skin the chicken drumsticks.
2. Mix together the breadcrumbs, grated cheese, garlic, paprika and salt.
3. Brush the chicken with the beaten egg then coat with the crumb mixture. Repeat with any remaining egg and crumbs.
4. Arrange the drumsticks on a suitable plate with the knuckles towards the centre.
5. Cook on the low rack on combination 200°C/MEDIUM for 15–18 min, until the coating is browned and crispy.

Left: Sausage Toad (page 36); below left: Queen of Puddings (page 42) centre: Fruit Crumble (page 38) right: Chicken and Ham Pie (page 37)

Family favourites

Family favourites

Sausage toad

(serves 4) colour page 34

COMBINATION: 200°C/LOW (30%)

This dish works well in combination cookers with continuous microwave energy

450g/1lb sausages
1 egg
275ml/10fl oz milk
1×5ml/tsp made mustard
125g/4oz flour
pinch salt
1×5ml/tsp dried mixed herbs

1. Prick the sausages well and place them in a suitable casserole dish. Cook for 10 min on the low rack on combination 200°C/LOW, re-arranging the sausages half way through cooking.
2. Prepare the batter by blending together the egg, milk and mustard in a liquidiser or processor and then adding the flour, salt and herbs. Mix to a smooth batter.
3. Pour the batter over the hot sausages. Cook for a further 20–25 min on combination 200°C/LOW until the batter is browned and crispy.
4. Serve immediately with freshly boiled cabbage or baked beans.

Cheesy haddock bake

(serves 4)

MICROWAVE: HIGH (100%)
COMBINATION: 180°C/MEDIUM (50%)

4 rashers streaky bacon, rinded
125g/4oz cheddar cheese, grated
2×15ml/tbsp tomato purée
4 haddock portions, approx 85g/3½oz each
4 tomatoes, halved

1. Place the bacon rashers on a microwave rack and cook for 3–4 min on microwave HIGH, until just becoming crispy. Cut into strips.
2. Combine the bacon with the cheese and tomato purée.
3. Place the haddock portions in a suitable shallow dish in a single layer and arrange the halved tomatoes around them. Top with the cheese and bacon mixture.
4. Cook on the low rack on combination 180°C/MEDIUM for 15–18 min if using fresh fish, or 20–25 min if using frozen, until the topping is melted and browned. Serve immediately with freshly cooked vegetables or salad.

Christmas turkey galantine

(serves 12) colour page 115

MICROWAVE: HIGH (100%)
COMBINATION: 180°C/MEDIUM (50%)

A boned turkey is easy to carve on Christmas Day, when there are always plenty of other things demanding attention. This recipe is delicious hot or cold

125g/4oz dried apricots
225g/8oz cranberries
125g/4oz caster sugar
150ml/5fl oz water
1 turkey, approx 4kg/8½lb
450g/1lb pork sausagemeat
4 thick slices tongue or ham, approx 225g/8oz in total
1 small onion, finely chopped
125g/4oz breadcrumbs
50g/2oz almonds, chopped
1×15ml/tbsp freshly chopped rosemary or 1×5ml/tsp dried
salt and pepper
1 egg, beaten

1. Place the apricots in a small dish, cover with water and then cover the dish. Heat on microwave HIGH for 5 min then allow to stand for 10 min. Drain and chop the apricots.
2. Place the cranberries, sugar and water in a covered dish and cook on microwave HIGH for 5–6 min until soft. Rub the cranberries and the juice through a nylon sieve and reserve the purée.
3. Bone the turkey completely, cutting down the backbone and cutting the meat away from the bones. Cut the rib cage away from the breast very carefully to prevent cutting the skin over

the breast. Lay the turkey on a chopping board, ready for stuffing.

4 Divide the sausagemeat into 2 and shape into 2 flat strips. Flour your hands if necessary, to prevent the sausagemeat from sticking. Place one strip on each breast of the turkey. Lay the slices of tongue or ham over the sausagemeat.
5 Complete the stuffing by combining the onion, breadcrumbs, chopped almonds, apricots, rosemary, salt and pepper. Mix well then add the beaten egg.
6 Lay the stuffing down the centre of the turkey, then draw the two sides together and truss the bird with string, making a roll of boneless meat.
7 Weigh the turkey, place on a large plate on the low rack and cook on combination 180°C/MEDIUM, allowing 7 min per 450g/lb.
8 20 min before the end of cooking, brush the turkey with a little of the cranberry glaze.
9 Serve the turkey hot or cold, with the remaining cranberry purée.

Cook's note: *Only 7 min per 450g/1lb instead of 9–11 min are required for this large boned turkey*

Macaroni cheese

(serves 4)

MICROWAVE: HIGH (100%)
COMBINATION: 200°C/MEDIUM (50%)

225g/8oz macaroni, or other pasta shapes
1×15ml/tbsp oil
salt
50g/2oz butter or margarine
1 large onion, chopped
50g/2oz flour
550ml/1pt milk
pepper
1×15ml/tbsp made mustard (optional)
75–125g/3–4oz cheddar cheese, grated

1 Bring a large pan of water to the boil on the hob, add the pasta, oil and a pinch of salt then cook for 10 min, or as directed on the packet. Drain.
2 While the macaroni is cooking, melt the butter in a suitable casserole dish for 1½–2min, on microwave HIGH. Add the onion and cook, covered, for 2–3 min.
3 Stir the flour into the dish, then gradually add the milk. Heat for 6–8 min, or until boiling and thickened, stirring every minute.
4 Season the sauce to taste with salt and pepper, adding the mustard, if used. Stir in most of the cheese.
5 Add the drained macaroni to the sauce, stirring well, then sprinkle with the remaining cheese.
6 Cook for 20–25 min on the low rack on combination 200°C/MEDIUM, until bubbling and browned. Serve with freshly cooked vegetables or a salad.

Cook's note: *The macaroni may be cooked in boiling water, covered, for 8 min on microwave HIGH*

Chicken and ham pie

(serves 6–8) *colour page 35*

MICROWAVE: HIGH (100%)
COMBINATION: 200°C/MEDIUM (50%)

This is a good way of using up left-overs from Christmas

50g/2oz butter or margarine
50g/2oz flour
550ml/1pt milk
salt and pepper
2×5ml/tsp capers (optional)
675g/1½lb cooked chicken and ham, mixed, chopped

for the pastry:
175g/6oz flour
pinch salt
75g/3oz butter or margarine
water to mix

1 Melt the butter in a suitable large casserole dish, for 1–2 min on microwave HIGH. Stir in the flour then gradually add the milk.
2 Heat for 6 min, or until boiled and thickened, stirring every minute. Season to taste with salt and pepper, add the capers, if used, then allow to cool. Stir in the chopped meats and insert a pie funnel into the centre of the dish.
3 Prepare the pastry by placing the flour and salt in a bowl, then rubbing in the butter or margarine until the mixture resembles fine breadcrumbs. Add sufficient water to mix to a firm dough.
4 Roll out the pastry and use to cover the pie. Make a small slit in the pastry crust and use any pastry trimmings for decoration. Cook for 20 min on the low rack on combination 200°C/MEDIUM until the pastry is browned and crisp.
5 Serve hot or cold.

Pineapple pudding

(serves 6) colour opposite

MICROWAVE: HIGH (100%)
COMBINATION: 180–190°C/LOW (30%)

8 canned pineapple rings, drained and juice reserved
25g/1oz glacé cherries
175g/6oz butter or margarine
175g/6oz caster sugar
3 eggs, beaten
175g/6oz self-raising flour
milk

1. Lightly oil a 1 litre/2pt pudding basin and arrange 6 of the drained pineapple rings around the sides and on the base. Place half a glacé cherry in the centre of each ring.
2. Cream together the butter or margarine and the caster sugar, until pale and fluffy. Gradually add the beaten eggs then fold in the flour. Add sufficient milk to give a soft dropping consistency.
3. Pile the sponge mixture into the basin and level the surface.
4. Cook on the low rack on combination 180–190°C/LOW for 15–18 min.
5. Leave for 2–3 min before turning onto a warmed plate.
6. While the pudding is standing, place the remaining pineapple rings, cherries, chopped, and the pineapple juice in a small bowl. Heat for 2 min on microwave HIGH.
7. Turn the pudding out onto a serving plate and serve with the sauce.

Fruit crumble

(serves 4) colour page 35

COMBINATION: 200°C/MEDIUM (50%)

675g/1½lb fruit, eg pears, apples, plums, rhubarb, etc
50–125g/2–4oz sugar, to taste
175g/6oz flour
75g/3oz butter or margarine
50g/2oz demerara sugar
demerara sugar for dredging

1. Prepare the fruits as necessary – peel apples and pears, trim and slice rhubarb etc. Place in the bottom of a serving dish with the sugar.
2. Place the flour in a bowl and rub in the butter or margarine until the mixture resembles fine breadcrumbs. Stir in the sugar.
3. Spoon the crumble over the fruit and sprinkle with a little extra demerara sugar.
4. Cook, uncovered, for 18–20 min on the low rack on combination 200°C/MEDIUM, until the crumble is set. Serve with custard or cream.

Steak and kidney pie

(serves 6) colour opposite

MICROWAVE: HIGH (100%)
COMBINATION: 160°C/LOW (30%) and 200°C/MEDIUM (50%)

2×15ml/tbsp oil
1 large onion, sliced
675g/1½lb stewing steak, cut into small pieces
225g/8oz lamb's kidneys, cored and cut into small pieces
2×15ml/tbsp flour
275ml/10fl oz boiling stock
salt and pepper

for the pastry:
175g/6oz flour
75g/3oz butter or margarine
water to mix
beaten egg to glaze

1. Heat the oil in a large suitable casserole dish for 2 min on microwave HIGH. Add the onion and cook, covered, for 4 min. Stir once during cooking.
2. Toss the steak and kidney in the flour and add to the casserole. Cover and cook for 6–8 min, stirring once.
3. Add the boiling stock and seasoning. Cover the dish and place on the low rack. Cook on combination 160°C/LOW for 1–1¼ hr, until the meat is tender. Season to taste then allow to cool. Transfer the meat to a pie dish, if preferred.
4. Place the flour for the pastry in a bowl and rub in the butter or margarine, until the mixture resembles fine breadcrumbs. Add sufficient water to give a stiff dough.
5. Roll out the pastry and use to cover the meat. Brush the pastry with beaten egg to glaze.
6. Cook on combination 200°C/MEDIUM for 20–25 min, until the pastry is browned and crisp. Serve with freshly cooked vegetables.

Pineapple Pudding (above); Steak and Kidney Pie (above); Baked Potatoes (page 92)

Honey roast lamb
(serves 6–8)

COMBINATION: 180°C/LOW (30%)

This is a traditional Welsh way of cooking lamb

1 leg lamb, approx 1.5kg/3½lb
1 sprig fresh rosemary
225g/8oz clear honey
150ml/5fl oz cider

1. Place the lamb in a shallow dish that will fit easily in the cooker. Make several slits in the meat and place a few pieces of rosemary in each.
2. Pour the honey over the joint and then add the cider.
3. Cook on the low rack on combination 180°C/LOW, allowing 20 min per 450g/lb. Baste the joint occasionally during cooking with the honey and cider.
4. Allow the lamb to stand for 5 min before carving and serving.

Cook's note: *Choose as square a leg of lamb as possible, particularly if you have a model with a turntable*

Honey roast gammon
(serves 12) *colour page 115*

MICROWAVE: HIGH (100%)
COMBINATION: 180°C/LOW (30%)

Roast gammon is a favourite at Christmas time but is also popular in the summer for slicing and serving with salads

1 unsmoked, boneless gammon joint, approx 1.8kg/4lb
4×15ml/tbsp clear honey
1 lemon, grated rind
2×15ml/tbsp demerara sugar

1. Soak the gammon overnight in cold water then drain. Weigh the soaked joint. Place the gammon in a covered dish on the low rack.
2. Cook the gammon on combination 180°C/LOW, allowing 18 min per 450g/lb. Turn the joint once during cooking.
3. 20 min before the end of the cooking period, remove the rind from the joint and score the fat.
4. Heat the honey, lemon rind and sugar together in a small bowl for 1 min on microwave HIGH. Brush over the gammon fat.
5. Cook for the remaining 20 min on combination 180°C/LOW, uncovered. Baste the gammon with the honey mixture occasionally.
6. Allow to cool then chill before slicing and serving cold.

Liver and bacon casserole
(serves 4)

MICROWAVE: HIGH (100%)
COMBINATION: 180°C/MEDIUM (50%)

2×15ml/tbsp oil
225g/8oz prepared mixed vegetables, eg leek, onion, parsnip, swede etc
675g/1½lb lamb's liver, sliced

Eve's pudding
(serves 6)

COMBINATION: 190°C/MEDIUM (50%)

This sponge pudding with fresh fruit makes a pleasant change from the more traditional syrup or dried fruit puddings

450g/1lb cooking apples, peeled, cored and sliced
50–75g/2–3oz sugar, to taste
125g/4oz butter or margarine
125/4oz caster sugar
2 eggs, beaten
few drops vanilla essence
125g/4oz self-raising flour
milk

1. Lightly grease a large ovenproof dish and place the prepared apples in the base. Sprinkle with sugar to taste.
2. Cream together the butter or margarine with the caster sugar until pale and fluffy, then gradually add the beaten eggs and vanilla essence. Fold in the flour then add sufficient milk to make a very soft dropping consistency.
3. Spread the cake mixture over the apples and smooth the surface.
4. Cook for 12 min on the low rack on combination 180–190°C/MEDIUM, until the sponge is set and lightly golden brown.
5. Serve hot with custard or cream.

Cooking for one or two

Above: Pork Chops with Kumquats (page 48)
left: Peanut and Stilton Cannelloni (page 48); right: Trout with Grapefruit and Ginger (page 48)

Cooking for one or two

Peanut and stilton cannelloni

(serves 2) colour page 46

MICROWAVE: HIGH (100%)
COMBINATION: 180°C/MEDIUM (50%)

This is a vegetarian dish. Dry roasted or traditionally roasted peanuts may be used, or a mixture of both

1 medium onion, finely chopped
1 clove garlic, crushed
2 tomatoes, skinned and chopped
50g/2oz mushrooms, finely chopped
50g/2oz salted peanuts
salt and pepper
6 easy-cook cannelloni tubes
20g/¾oz butter or margarine
20g/¾oz flour
275ml/10fl oz milk
50g/2oz stilton, crumbled

for garnish: parsley sprigs

1. Place the onion and garlic in a small covered dish and cook on microwave HIGH for 2 min. Add the tomatoes and mushrooms and cook for 5 min, uncovered.
2. Stir the peanuts into the tomato sauce and season to taste then use the mixture to fill the cannelloni tubes. Place in a small casserole dish.
3. Heat the butter or margarine for 30–60 sec until melted then stir in the flour. Gradually add the milk then heat for 4–5 min on microwave HIGH until boiling and thickened, stirring every minute.
4. Add most of the stilton to the sauce then add salt and pepper to taste. Pour over the cannelloni and top with the remaining cheese.
5. Cook on the low rack on combination 180°C/MEDIUM for 15 min.
6. For extra browning use grill combination medium for 2–3 min or place under a conventional grill.
7. Serve hot with a side salad and garnish with parsley sprigs.

Cook's note: *Use the handle of a teaspoon to push the filling into the cannelloni tubes*

Trout with grapefruit and ginger

(serves 2) colour page 47

COMBINATION: 200°C/LOW (30%)

2 trout, weighing approx 350g/12oz each, cleaned
1 grapefruit, grated rind and juice
1 small piece fresh ginger, peeled and finely grated
freshly ground black pepper

for serving: parsley butter and watercress

1. Trim and wash the trout. Place in a suitable serving dish.
2. Mix together the grapefruit rind and ginger and place half the mixture in the cavity of each fish. Pour the grapefruit juice over. Sprinkle with pepper.
3. Cook on the low rack on combination 200°C/LOW for 10 min, or until the trout are cooked.
4. Garnish each trout with a knob of parsley butter, add some watercress and serve.

Cook's note: *Rainbow trout are black in colour when first caught. They only take on their attractive pinky-green appearance when they have been exposed to the air for a little while*

Pork chops with kumquats

(serves 2) colour page 46

MICROWAVE: HIGH (100%)
COMBINATION: 180°C/LOW (30%)

1 small onion, finely sliced
1 small piece fresh ginger, peeled and grated
125g/4oz kumquats, washed
1×15ml/tbsp freshly chopped sage
2 pork chops, each weighing approx 225g/8oz
salt and pepper
275ml/10fl oz boiling vegetable stock
1×15ml/tbsp demerara sugar

1. Place the onion and ginger in a covered casserole dish and cook for 2 min on microwave HIGH. Add the kumquats and sage and cook for a further 2 min.
2. Lay the chops on the kumquat and onion mixture and season with salt and pepper. Pour

Chicken à la grecque

(serves 1)

MICROWAVE: HIGH (100%)
COMBINATION: 200°C/MEDIUM (50%)

1×15ml/tbsp olive oil
1 clove garlic, crushed
1 lemon, grated rind
50g/2oz small button mushrooms
2 tomatoes, skinned and chopped
1×15ml/tbsp freshly chopped oregano
salt and pepper
1×275g/10oz chicken portion

for garnish: chopped parsley

1. Heat the oil in a suitable casserole dish for 1 min on microwave HIGH. Add the garlic, lemon rind, mushrooms, tomatoes, oregano and salt and pepper. Cook for 5 min on microwave HIGH.
2. Add the chicken portion to the dish and spoon the sauce over the chicken. Cover and cook on the low rack on combination 200°C/MEDIUM for 15 min, until the chicken is tender.
3. Remove the chicken to a serving plate with the mushrooms. Sieve the sauce then heat for 2 min on microwave HIGH. Spoon the sauce over the chicken and serve with freshly cooked vegetables or a mixed salad.

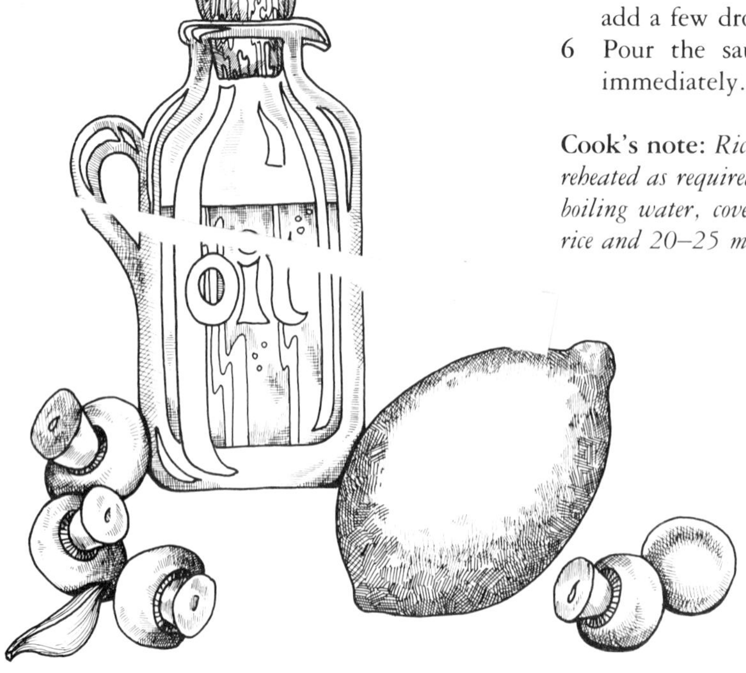

Kidneys with sherry and sweetcorn

(serves 1)

MICROWAVE: HIGH (100%)
COMBINATION: 180°C/LOW (30%)

25g/1oz butter or margarine
1 small onion, finely sliced
225g/8oz lamb's kidneys, cored and chopped
1×5ml/tsp freshly chopped sage
salt and pepper
3×15ml/tbsp sherry
2–3×15ml/tbsp sweetcorn kernels or 4–5 miniature corn cobs, fresh or canned
1×15ml/tbsp single cream
worcestershire sauce

for serving: freshly cooked rice

1. Heat the butter or margarine in a small casserole dish for 1 min on microwave HIGH. Add the onion and cook, covered, for 2 min.
2. Add the kidneys, sage, salt, pepper and sherry to the dish and cook, covered, for 12–15 min on the low rack on combination 180°C/LOW.
3. Add the sweetcorn to the dish and cook on combination 180°C/LOW for a further 10 min.
4. Remove the kidneys and corn to a bed of freshly cooked rice. Heat the juices for 3 min on microwave HIGH until reduced and slightly thickened.
5. Add the cream to the sauce, season to taste and add a few drops of worcestershire sauce.
6. Pour the sauce over the kidneys and serve immediately.

Cook's note: *Rice may be cooked in the microwave and reheated as required. Cook 225g/8oz rice in 550ml/1pt boiling water, covered, allowing 12–15 min for white rice and 20–25 min for brown on 100% power*

Pheasant chasseur

(serves 2)

MICROWAVE: HIGH (100%)
COMBINATION: 200°C/LOW (30%)

65g/2½oz butter
1 pheasant, cut into halves
1 onion, finely sliced
1 clove garlic, crushed
175g/6oz mushrooms, sliced
salt and pepper
275ml/10fl oz red wine
125g/4oz baby onions, peeled

for garnish: freshly chopped parsley

1. Melt 25g/1oz of the butter in a casserole dish for 1–2 min on microwave HIGH. Brush a little of the butter over the pheasant.
2. Add the onion and garlic to the remaining melted butter and cook, covered, for 2 min on microwave HIGH. Add the pheasant halves, mushrooms, salt and pepper and red wine. Cover and cook on the low rack on combination 200°C/LOW for 20 min.
3. While the pheasant is cooking, melt the remaining butter in a small frying pan on the hob and fry the baby onions until browned and soft.
4. Add the onions to the casserole and cook for a further 10 min, uncovered, on the low rack on combination 200°C/LOW.
5. Serve the pheasant with the sauce spooned over.

Cook's note: *If no hob is available, melt 40g/1½oz butter on microwave HIGH for 1–2 min. Cook the onions in the butter, covered, for 3–4 min, then leave until required, while following the recipe as above*

Cod and broccoli mornay

(serves 2)

MICROWAVE: HIGH (100%)
COMBINATION: 200°C/MEDIUM (50%)

225g/8oz small broccoli heads
3×15ml/tbsp water
25g/1oz butter or margarine
25g/1oz flour
275ml/10fl oz milk
75g/3oz cheddar cheese, grated
salt and pepper
450g/1lb filleted cod, skinned

1. Wash the broccoli and shake dry. Place in a covered microwave casserole dish with the water and cook for 5 min on microwave HIGH, stirring once. Leave covered until required.
2. Melt the butter in a dish or bowl for 1 min then stir in the flour. Gradually add the milk and any water from the broccoli. Heat for 4–5 min, stirring every minute, until boiling and thickened.
3. Add most of the cheese to the sauce and then season to taste.
4. Arrange the cod around the sides of a 1 litre/2pt casserole dish, and place the broccoli in the centre of the dish. Pour the sauce over and sprinkle with the remaining cheese.
5. Cook on the low rack on combination 200°C/MEDIUM for 15-18 min. Serve with sliced tomato.

Duckling with guava and mango

(serves 1)

MICROWAVE: HIGH (100%)
COMBINATION: 200°C/LOW (30%)

Guavas and mangoes should be used when they are ripe to get their full flavour. Buy when they are firm and ripen at home in a warm place, such as the airing cupboard

1 small onion, finely chopped
1 small guava, peeled and chopped
1 small mango, peeled and diced
1 duckling portion, 400–450g/14–16oz
salt and pepper

1. Place the onion, guava and mango in a small covered casserole dish and cook on microwave HIGH for 4 min. Stir once during cooking.
2. Prick the skin of the duckling thoroughly and rub salt into the skin. Lay the duckling on the fruits.
3. Cook, uncovered, on the low rack on combination 200°C/LOW for 20 min, until the duck is tender and the skin browned.
4. Remove the duck to a warmed serving plate. Strain any excess fat from the fruits in the casserole dish then season to taste with salt and pepper.
5. Rub the sauce through a sieve and pour over the duck. Serve immediately with freshly cooked vegetables or a salad.

Baked lamb with fig and orange sauce

(serves 1) colour opposite

MICROWAVE: HIGH (100%)
COMBINATION: 180°C/LOW (30%)

3 large dried figs
cold water to cover
1 small orange
1 small onion, finely chopped
1 lamb leg bone steak, approx
275g/10oz, boned
salt and pepper
demerara sugar (optional)

for garnish: fresh fig
for serving: freshly cooked vegetables

1. Place the dried figs in a small covered dish, cover with cold water and cook on microwave HIGH for 4 min. Leave to stand, covered, for 10 min, then drain the figs, reserving the liquid. Chop the figs finely.
2. Finely pare the rind from part of the orange and cut into thin strips for garnish. Grate the remaining rind then squeeze the juice from the orange.
3. Cook the onion in a small covered casserole with 1×15ml/tbsp orange juice for 2 min. Add the lamb and cook for 3 min.
4. Add sufficient of the fig water to the orange juice to yield 150ml/5fl oz. Season the lamb with salt and pepper, sprinkle with the chopped figs and grated orange rind then pour the juice over. Cover and cook on the low rack on combination 180°C/LOW for 10 min. Preheat the conventional grill.
5. Remove the leg bone steak to the grill pan and cook slowly to brown while the sauce is being completed.
6. Rub the sauce through a coarse sieve then heat on microwave HIGH for 5 min, or until well reduced and thickened. Season to taste, adding a little sugar if required.
7. Serve the leg bone steak with the sauce over, sprinkled with the shredded orange peel. Serve a selection of freshly cooked vegetables. Garnish with a fresh fig, if in season.

Cook's note: *Leg bone steaks or gigot chops are a good way of buying lean lamb to cook for one person. It is simply a slice through the leg of the lamb. Combination settings (page 16) or grill combination, where available, may be used to cook the lamb*

Curried chicken pilaf

(serves 2)

MICROWAVE: HIGH (100%)
COMBINATION: 180°C/MEDIUM (50%)

25g/1oz butter or margarine
1 small onion, finely sliced
½ red pepper, sliced
1 clove garlic, crushed
½–1×5ml/tsp curry powder, to taste
225g/8oz chicken breasts, cut into strips
125g/4oz easy-cook long grain rice
25g/1oz raisins
275ml/10fl oz boiling vegetable stock
1 banana, thickly sliced
few drops lemon juice

for garnish: freshly chopped parsley

1. Place the butter in a suitable casserole dish and heat for 1 min on microwave HIGH. Add the onion, pepper, garlic and curry powder and cook, covered, for 3 min.
2. Add the chicken strips to the dish and cook, covered, for a further 3 min, stirring once.
3. Stir the rice, raisins and stock into the dish, and cook, covered, for 18–20 min on the low rack on combination 180°C/MEDIUM, until the stock is absorbed.
4. Allow the dish to stand for 5 min, then season to taste with salt and pepper. Dip the banana in the lemon juice and arrange around the pilaf then garnish with some freshly chopped parsley. Serve immediately.

Baked Lamb with Fig and Orange Sauce (above); Shortbread (page 113)

CHIC TO CHIC
Studied looks, left,
wearing a cotton
jersey, polo neck top
(£60) and a brown
wool, striped jacket
(£163), both by Nicole
Farhi for Stephen
Marks. Grey flannel
skirt with back flap
(£47.95) by
Barnett

Prawn and almond bass

(serves 2)

COMBINATION: 200°C/MEDIUM (50%)

Bass is a delicious but expensive luxury. By adding prawns the bass can be stretched to go a little further, and the resulting dish is still a treat

2 small fillets of bass, approx 225g/8oz each
40g/1½oz blanched almonds, chopped
1×15ml/tbsp chopped chives
175g/6oz peeled prawns
salt
white pepper
1×15ml/tbsp lemon juice
15g/½oz butter, cut into slivers

1 Place the bass fillets in a shallow ovenproof glass dish.
2 Mix together the blanched almonds, chives, prawns, salt and pepper. Scatter over the bass. Sprinkle with the lemon juice and dot with the butter.
3 Cook on the low rack on combination 200°C/MEDIUM for 10 min, until the top is slightly crisp. Serve with freshly cooked vegetables or a side salad with watercress.

Veal in cream with okra

(serves 1–2)

MICROWAVE: HIGH (100%)
COMBINATION: 160°C/LOW (30%)

Veal and okra seem an unusual combination, but they mix well in this dish, which is a real treat. It is rich, so will serve 1–2, depending on appetites

25g/1oz butter or margarine
75g/3oz okra, trimmed and washed
225g/8oz veal escalope, cut into strips
1×15ml/tbsp fine wholewheat flour
3×15ml/tbsp dubonnet
2×15ml/tbsp soured cream
salt and pepper

for garnish: freshly chopped parsley

1 Melt the butter or margarine in a suitable casserole dish for 1 min on microwave HIGH. Add the okra and cook, covered, for 2 min.
2 Toss the veal in the flour then add to the dish and cook, covered, for 3 min, stirring once.
3 Add the dubonnet to the casserole and cook, covered, for 15 min on the low rack on combination 160°C/LOW.
4 Stir in the cream then season to taste with salt and pepper. Sprinkle with chopped parsley and serve immediately with fresh green vegetables.

Vegetarian and wholefood dishes

Above: Lentil and Mushroom Lasagne (page 61) below left: Chick Peas in White Wine with Mushrooms (page 60); centre: Poacher's Pot (page 61); right: Spiced Pork with Celery and Bananas (page 60)

Vegetarian and wholefood dishes

Chick peas in white wine with mushrooms

(serves 6) colour page 58

MICROWAVE: HIGH (100%)
COMBINATION: 180°C/MEDIUM (50%)

A perfect wholefood dish for entertaining or any special occasion. This dish will be enjoyed by vegetarians and meat-eaters alike

275g/10oz chick peas
2 large onions, sliced
1 clove garlic, crushed
2 stalks celery, chopped
1 red pepper, deseeded and cut into strips
2 courgettes, sliced
225g/8oz mushrooms, sliced
275ml/10fl oz dry white wine
275ml/10fl oz boiling vegetable stock (approx)
2×15ml/tbsp freshly chopped tarragon or 2×5ml/tsp dried tarragon
salt and freshly ground black pepper
150ml/5fl oz soured cream

for garnish: chopped tarragon

1 Place the chick peas in a large microwave dish and cover with boiling water. Cover the dish and heat for 5 min on microwave HIGH, then leave to soak for 1 hr.
2 Drain and rinse the chick peas. Cover with fresh boiling water, cover the dish and cook for a further 15 min on microwave HIGH. Set to one side, covered, until required.
3 Place the onions, garlic and celery in a suitable 1.5 litre/3pt casserole dish and cook for 6 min on microwave HIGH, stirring once.
4 Add the red pepper, courgettes and mushrooms to the dish and cook for a further 6 min, stirring once.
5 Drain the chick peas and add them to the casserole with the wine, stock and seasonings. Cover and cook on the low rack on combination 180°C/MEDIUM for 40 min, or until the chick peas are tender.
6 Season the chick peas with salt and pepper. If necessary, cook uncovered for 5–10 min on microwave HIGH to reduce the cooking liquor.
7 Stir the soured cream into the chick peas then serve, garnished with a little extra tarragon.

Cook's note: *If preparing this in advance of a dinner party or similar occasion, stop at the end of step 5 and allow the dish to cool. Reheat before serving on microwave* HIGH, *then stir in the soured cream. Heat for a further 2–3 min if necessary*

Spiced pork with celery and banana

(serves 4) colour page 59

MICROWAVE: HIGH (100%)
COMBINATION: 180°C/MEDIUM (50%)

Dried bananas are often used in muesli mixes. Here they are used to add a slightly sweet flavour to a pork casserole

2×15ml/tbsp oil
1 onion, finely sliced
1 clove garlic, crushed
4 stalks celery, chopped
450g/1lb pork fillet, cut into thin slices
1×15ml/tbsp wholewheat flour
2×5ml/tsp ground cumin
1×5ml/tsp ground ginger
425ml/15fl oz boiling stock
salt and pepper
50g/2oz dried banana chips
1×15ml/tbsp chopped parsley

1 Heat the oil in a casserole dish for 2 min on microwave HIGH, add the onion and garlic and cook, covered, for 3 min. Add the celery and cook for a further 6 min, stirring once.
2 Toss the pork fillet in the flour and spices, then add to the vegetables with the remaining flour and spices. Cook, covered, for a further 4 min on microwave HIGH.
3 Pour the boiling stock into the casserole and add some salt and pepper. Cover and cook for 20 min on the low rack on combination 180°C/MEDIUM.
4 Stir the banana chips and parsley into the casserole and cook for a further 15 min. Season to taste and serve.

Poacher's pot

(serves 4) colour page 58

MICROWAVE: HIGH (100%)
COMBINATION: 160°C/LOW (30%)

1 pheasant, cut into joints
½ rabbit, jointed, or 350g/12oz boneless diced rabbit
350g/12oz boneless stewing venison
2×15ml/tbsp oil
1 leek, cut into rings
2 large onions, sliced
1 large carrot, sliced
225g/8oz swede, diced
2×15ml/tbsp wholewheat flour
275ml/10fl oz red wine
salt and pepper
1–2×15ml/tbsp mustard seeds
2 bay leaves
2×15ml/tbsp freshly chopped rosemary
225g/8oz flat mushrooms, sliced
for the marinade:
1 large onion, finely sliced
salt and freshly ground black pepper
2 bay leaves
3×15ml/tbsp oil
3×15ml/tbsp red wine vinegar
425ml/15fl oz red wine
for garnish: fresh rosemary

1 Mix together the prepared game and place in a bowl with all the marinade ingredients. Stir carefully then leave in a cool place to marinade for at least 8 hr. Stir once or twice whilst marinading.
2 Heat the oil in a large casserole dish for 2 min on microwave HIGH, add the leek, onion, carrot and swede and cook, covered, for 6 min, stirring once.
3 Remove the game from the marinade, then strain and reserve the liquid.
4 Sprinkle the flour over the meat, then add to the vegetables and cook, covered, for 6 min on microwave HIGH, stirring once.
5 Add sufficient red wine to the reserved marinade to make 550ml/1pt. Add the salt and pepper, mustard seeds, bay leaves and rosemary to the casserole then add the liquid.
5 Cover and cook for 1½ hr on the low rack on combination 160°C/LOW, until the game is tender.
6 Slice the mushrooms and add them to the casserole. Adjust the seasoning and cook for a further 15 min.
7 Garnish with fresh rosemary before serving.

Lentil and mushroom lasagne

(serves 6) colour page 58

MICROWAVE: HIGH (100%)
COMBINATION: 200°C/MEDIUM (50%)

This vegetarian lasagne makes a pleasant change from the traditional minced beef version

350g/12oz red lentils, washed
850ml/1½pt boiling vegetable stock
2×15ml/tbsp oil
1 large onion, finely sliced
2 cloves garlic, crushed
2 sticks celery, finely chopped
400g/14oz can chopped tomatoes
275ml/10fl oz red wine
salt and freshly ground black pepper
50g/2oz butter
450g/1lb mushrooms, sliced
8 sheets easy-cook lasagne
25g/1oz butter or margarine
25g/1oz flour
150ml/5fl oz milk
150ml/5fl oz single cream
1×5ml/tsp wholegrain mustard
50g/2oz cheddar cheese, grated

1 Place the lentils in a large bowl with the stock. Cover and cook for 20 min on microwave HIGH, until the lentils are soft and form a thick purée.
2 Place the oil, onion, 1 clove of garlic and the celery in a large bowl, cover and cook for 5 min on HIGH, stirring once. Add the lentils, tomatoes, red wine, salt and pepper. Cook, uncovered, for 15 min on microwave HIGH. Leave until required.
3 Melt the butter in a large casserole dish for 1–2 min on microwave HIGH, add the other garlic clove and the sliced mushrooms, cover and cook for 5 min. Season with black pepper.
4 Place half the lentil mixture in the base of a 1.5 litre/3pt dish, cover with 4 of the lasagne sheets then top with half the mushrooms. Repeat the layers.
5 Melt the butter or margarine on microwave HIGH for 1 min. Add the flour then gradually stir in the milk. Heat for 2–3 min, stirring every minute, on HIGH. Add the cream and mustard then season to taste.
6 Pour the sauce over the lasagne then top with the grated cheese.
7 Cook, uncovered, on the low rack on combination 200°C/MEDIUM for 25 min, until the cheese is well browned.

Bacon and mushroom loaf

(serves 4) colour opposite

MICROWAVE: HIGH (100%)
COMBINATION: 180°C/MEDIUM (50%)

This loaf travels well and is ideal for summer picnics

225g/8oz streaky bacon, derinded
2×15ml/tbsp oil
1 onion, finely chopped
1 clove garlic, crushed
2 stalks celery, finely sliced
225g/8oz mushrooms, finely chopped
225g/8oz cold cooked rice
salt and pepper
½×5ml/tsp ground allspice
2×15ml/tbsp freshly chopped parsley
2 eggs, beaten

for garnish: salad

1. Arrange 4 rashers of bacon in the bottom of a 550ml/1pt ovenproof glass loaf dish. Finely chop the remaining rashers.
2. Heat the oil in a large microwave dish for 2 min on microwave HIGH, add the onion, garlic and celery and cook, covered, for 3 min. Stir in the chopped bacon and cook for a further 2 min, covered.
3. Add all the remaining ingredients and mix well, seasoning to taste. Spoon the mixture into the prepared loaf dish.
4. Cook on the low rack on combination 180°C/MEDIUM for 20 min, until lightly browned and set.
5. Ease the loaf away from the sides of the dish with a palette knife and turn out onto a warmed serving dish.
6. Garnish with a little salad and serve.

Bean and pepper stew

(serves 8) colour opposite

MICROWAVE: HIGH (100%)
COMBINATION: 180°C/MEDIUM (50%) and 200°C/MEDIUM (50%)

350g/12oz mixed dried beans
boiling water
2 large onions, sliced
2 cloves garlic, crushed
2 red peppers, deseeded and cut into strips
2 green peppers, deseeded and cut into strips
2×400g/14oz cans chopped tomatoes
2×15ml/tbsp tomato purée
salt and freshly ground black pepper
2×15ml/tbsp freshly chopped mixed herbs or 2×5ml/tsp dried mixed herbs
275ml/10fl oz red wine or stock (approx)
125g/4oz cheddar cheese, grated

1. Place the beans in a large microwave bowl. Cover with boiling water then cover the bowl and cook for 15 min on microwave HIGH. Allow to stand for one hour or until required.
2. Place the onion, garlic and peppers in a large ovenproof glass bowl or casserole dish. Cover and cook for 10 min on microwave HIGH, stirring once. Drain the beans and stir into the vegetables.
3. Add the chopped tomatoes, tomato purée, and seasonings, with sufficient wine or stock to cover the beans. Cover the dish and cook for 1 hr, or until the beans are cooked, on the low rack on combination 180°C/MEDIUM.
4. Season the beans to taste then scatter the cheese over the top. Cook for a further 10–15 min on the low rack on combination 200°C/MEDIUM, until the cheese is melted and browned.
5. Serve with crusty bread and a side salad.

Pinto pancake torte

(serves 4) colour opposite

MICROWAVE: HIGH (100%) and MEDIUM (50%)
COMBINATION: 180°C/MEDIUM (50%)

This dish is based on a Mexican recipe. If you are unable to obtain enchilada sauce mix, add 1×5ml/tsp each of chilli powder and paprika to the tomato purée and 275ml/10fl oz water

225g/8oz pinto beans
boiling water
3×15ml/tbsp oil plus oil for frying
1 large onion, chopped
1 clove garlic, crushed
1 red pepper, seeded and cut into strips
½–1×5ml/tsp chilli powder
400g/14oz can chopped tomatoes
salt and freshly ground black pepper
1 egg

Bean and Pepper Stew (above); Bacon and Mushroom Loaf (above); Pinto Pancake Torte (above)

275ml/10fl oz milk
125g/4oz flour
1×39g/1.38oz pkt enchilada sauce mix
275ml/10fl oz water
175g/6oz tomato purée
75g/3oz cheddar cheese, grated
2 medium avocados
juice ½ lemon
150ml/5fl oz soured cream

1 Place the beans in a large bowl and cover with boiling water. Cover the bowl and heat for 10 min on microwave HIGH. Allow to stand for 1 hr.
2 Drain and rinse the beans. Return them to the bowl and cover with fresh boiling water. Cover the bowl and cook for 15 min on microwave HIGH, then a further 15–20 min on microwave MEDIUM, until soft. Leave until required.
3 Heat the oil in a suitable dish on microwave HIGH for 1 min. Add the onion and garlic and cook, covered, for 3 min, stirring once. Add the red pepper and chilli powder, then cook for 4 min, stirring once.
4 Drain the pinto beans and place in a liquidiser or processor with the onion and pepper mixture and the canned tomatoes. Process to a smooth purée, then season to taste with salt and pepper.
5 Transfer the purée to a microwave dish and cook, uncovered, for 15 min, until slightly thickened.
6 While the purée is cooking, prepare and cook the pancakes. Place the egg and milk in a liquidiser or processor and blend together. Shoot in the flour with a pinch of salt and process until blended.
7 Heat a little oil in a small frying pan or omelet pan and use the batter to make 6 thick pancakes, adding more oil to the pan as necessary.
8 Lay one pancake in the bottom of a shallow ovenproof glass dish. Spread with a little of the pinto purée then repeat until all the purée and pancakes are used up. Finish with a pancake.
9 Make up the enchilada sauce as directed, with the tomato purée and water. Pour sufficient sauce over the pancake torte to cover, then sprinkle with the grated cheese. (Any remaining sauce may be frozen for later use.)
10 Cook on the low rack on combination 180°C/MEDIUM for 12–15 min, until the cheese is melted and browned.
11 While the torte is cooking, place the flesh from the avocados in a liquidiser or processor with the lemon juice and soured cream. Process to a smooth purée, season to taste then serve with the torte.

Cook's note: *Pinto beans are small brown beans widely used in Mexican cookery and are traditionally used in chilli con carne. Red kidney beans may be used as a substitute and will give a more colourful finished dish*

Butter bean goulash

(serves 4)

MICROWAVE: HIGH (100%)
COMBINATION: 180°C/MEDIUM (50%)

225g/8oz butter beans
boiling water
2×15ml/tbsp oil
2 large onions, sliced
2 cloves garlic
2 green peppers, deseeded and cut into strips
1×15ml/tbsp paprika
pinch cayenne pepper
2×15ml/tbsp tomato purée
150ml/5fl oz red wine
425ml/15fl oz boiling stock
salt and pepper
1×15ml/tbsp dark demerara sugar

1 Place the beans in a large bowl and cover with boiling water. Cover the bowl and heat for 10 min on microwave HIGH, then allow to stand for 1 hr. Drain and rinse the beans.
2 Return the beans to the bowl and cover with fresh boiling water. Cover the bowl and cook for 15 min on microwave HIGH. Remove from the cooker and leave until required.
3 Heat the oil in a large ovenproof glass bowl or casserole for 2 min on microwave HIGH. Add the onions and garlic and cook for a further 3 min.
4 Add the sliced peppers to the bowl and cook, covered, for 8 min on microwave HIGH, stirring once.
5 Drain the beans and add them to the bowl with the paprika, cayenne, tomato purée, wine, boiling stock, salt and pepper.
6 Cover the casserole and cook for 50–60 min on the low rack on combination 180°C/MEDIUM, until the beans are tender.
7 Add the sugar then adjust the seasoning to taste and serve with a side salad.

Cheese and vegetable pie
(serves 4)

MICROWAVE: HIGH (100%)
COMBINATION: 200°C/MEDIUM (50%)

A pastry lid turns a dish of vegetables in cheese sauce into a substantial main meal

675g/1½lb mixed prepared vegetables, eg carrots, onions, parsnips, leeks, courgettes, potatoes, etc
5×15ml/tbsp water

for the sauce:
40g/1½oz butter or margarine
40g/1½oz flour
425ml/15fl oz milk
50g/2oz cheddar cheese, grated
salt and pepper

for the pastry:
175g/6oz flour
pinch each salt and dry mustard
75g/3oz butter or margarine
50g/2oz cheddar cheese, finely grated
water

1. Place the prepared vegetables in a suitable dish and add the water. Cook, covered, on microwave HIGH, for 10–12 min, until just cooked. Stir once or twice during cooking. Leave until required.
2. Melt the butter or margarine for the sauce in a bowl, on microwave HIGH for 1 min. Stir in the flour then gradually add the milk. Heat for 4–5 min until boiling and thickened, stirring every minute.
3. Add the cheese to the sauce then season to taste with salt and pepper. Add the water from the vegetables then pour the sauce over the vegetables and mix well. Insert a pie funnel into the centre of the dish.
4. Prepare the pastry by placing the flour, salt and mustard powder in a bowl, then rubbing in the butter or margarine until the mixture resembles fine breadcrumbs. Stir in the cheese, then add sufficient cold water to bind to a stiff dough.
5. Roll out the pastry and use to cover the vegetable filling.
6. Cook on the low rack on combination 200°C/MEDIUM for 15–18 min, until the pastry is browned and crisp.
7. Serve hot or cold.

Spiced baked beans

(serves 4)

MICROWAVE: HIGH (100%)
COMBINATION: 180°C/MEDIUM (50%)

225g/8oz haricot beans
boiling water
1 onion, finely chopped
1×15ml/tbsp molasses
2×15ml/tbsp tomato purée
2×5ml/tsp dry mustard powder
2×5ml/tsp worcestershire sauce
1×5ml/tsp salt
225g/8oz spicy sausage, thickly sliced (optional)

for serving: white meat, poultry or salad

1 Place the beans in a bowl and cover with boiling water. Cover the dish and heat for 10 min on microwave HIGH. Allow to stand for 1 hr then drain and rinse the beans.
2 Return the beans to the dish and cover with fresh boiling water. Cover and heat for 15 min on microwave HIGH then leave until required.
3 Mix together the onion, molasses, tomato purée, mustard, worcestershire sauce and salt. Drain the beans and add to the mixture with sufficient water from the beans to cover.
4 Cover the dish and cook on the low rack on combination 180°C/MEDIUM for 30 min, until the beans are tender.
5 If using spicy sausage, add it to the dish and cook, covered, for a further 10 min. Serve with white meat, poultry, or a side salad.

Chicken marengo

(serves 4) colour opposite

MICROWAVE: HIGH (100%)
COMBINATION: 180°C/MEDIUM (50%)

Tradition has it that chicken marengo was created by Napoleon's chef to celebrate victory at the Battle of Marengo. The dish was made from the ingredients that the chef could find in the countryside. Some say that it should be garnished with fried eggs, others with crayfish

50g/2oz butter
3×15ml/tbsp olive oil
2 onions, finely sliced
1 clove garlic, crushed
1 large chicken, about 2kg/4½lb, cut into 8 portions and skinned
1×15ml/tbsp flour
150ml/5fl oz boiling chicken stock
275ml/10fl oz marsala or sherry
1×15ml/tbsp tomato purée
6 tomatoes, skinned and chopped
12 button mushrooms, finely sliced
salt and freshly ground black pepper
4×15ml/tbsp brandy

for garnish: crayfish or langoustines

1 Heat the butter and oil in a casserole dish for 2 min on microwave HIGH. Add the onions and garlic and cook, covered, for 4 min, stirring once.
2 Add the chicken joints to the casserole and cook for 6 min, stirring once. Remove the chicken from the casserole and set to one side. Add the flour to the onions then gradually stir in the stock, marsala and tomato purée.
3 Heat the sauce for 4–5 min on microwave HIGH, stirring every minute, or until boiling. Add the chicken joints and cook on the low rack on combination 180°C/MEDIUM for 15 min.
4 Add the tomatoes and mushrooms to the dish with salt and freshly ground black pepper. Cover and cook for a further 30 min on the low rack on combination 180°C/MEDIUM. Add the brandy and cook for another 10 min.
5 Season to taste, garnish and serve.

Gratin verde

(serves 6–8)

MICROWAVE: HIGH (100%)
COMBINATION: 200°C/MEDIUM (50%)

225g/8oz green tagliatelle
salt and pepper
1×15ml/tbsp oil
1 green pepper, deseeded and cut into strips
2 stalks celery, sliced
1 large leek, finely sliced
50g/2oz butter or margarine
50g/2oz flour
425ml/15fl oz milk
150ml/5fl oz set natural yogurt
1×5ml/tsp wholegrain mustard
50g/2oz cheddar cheese, grated

Chicken Marengo (above)

BORDEAUX SUPÉRIEUR
CHATEAU
1983

1. Bring a large pan of water to the boil on the hob. Add the tagliatelle, a pinch of salt and the oil and simmer for 10 min, or as directed. Drain and rinse in cold water.
2. Place the pepper, celery and leek in a covered microwave dish and cook for 6–8 min on microwave HIGH, until just cooked and still crisp. Stir once during cooking.
3. Melt the butter or margarine in a large jug or bowl for 1–2 min, then stir in the flour. Gradually add the milk then heat for 5–6 min on microwave HIGH until boiling and thick. Stir every minute.
4. Add the yogurt to the sauce with the mustard, then season to taste with salt and pepper. Combine the sauce with the tagliatelle and the cooked vegetables then turn into a large ovenproof casserole dish and sprinkle with the grated cheese.
5. Cook on the low rack on combination 200°C/MEDIUM for 20 min, until the cheese has melted and browned.

Cook's note: *The tagliatelle may be cooked in the combination cooker on microwave HIGH. Cook in 550ml/1pt boiling water for 5–6 min, covered*

Stir-fry quiche

(serves 6)

COMBINATION: 200°C/MEDIUM (50%) and 180°C/LOW (30%)

for the pastry:
175g/6oz wholewheat flour
pinch salt
75g/3oz butter or margarine
water to mix

for the filling:
125g/4oz mixed stir-fry vegetables, eg carrots, cabbage, mushrooms, sweetcorn, beansprouts, etc
230g/8oz can water chestnuts, drained
125g/4oz quark
150ml/5fl oz single cream
2 eggs, beaten
salt and pepper
2×15ml/tbsp soy sauce

for garnish: spring onion

1. Place the flour in a bowl with the salt, then rub in the butter or margarine until the mixture resembles fine breadcrumbs. Add sufficient water to mix to a firm dough. Knead gently on a lightly floured surface then roll out and use to line a 20cm/8in ovenproof glass flan dish. Prick the base of the pastry with a fork.
2. Line the pastry with greaseproof paper and fill with baking beans. Bake for 10 min on the low rack on combination 200°C/MEDIUM. Remove the paper and the beans from the dish.
3. Place the stir-fry vegetables and the water chestnuts in the pastry case. Beat together the quark, cream and eggs, then add salt and pepper to taste with the soy sauce. Pour the mixture into the pastry.
4. Cook for 15–18 min on the low rack on combination 180°C/LOW until set. Leave to cool slightly.
5. Garnish with spring onion and serve warm with stir-fry vegetables, or cold with salad.

Spiced herrings with pepper

(serves 4) *colour page 75*

COMBINATION: 200°C/MEDIUM (50%)

Herrings seem somewhat neglected now that we have such a large selection of fresh fish available to choose from. This is a tasty and attractive way of serving an old favourite

4 large herrings, cleaned, approx 225g/8oz each
1 small green pepper, deseeded and sliced
1 small red pepper, deseeded and sliced
small piece fresh ginger, peeled and grated
2×15ml/tbsp tomato purée
1×15ml/tbsp demerara sugar
3×15ml/tbsp dry sherry
2×15ml/tbsp naturally fermented soy sauce
2×5ml/tsp ground ginger
150ml/5fl oz water

1. Place the prepared herrings in a suitable casserole dish and scatter the sliced peppers and grated ginger over the fish.
2. Mix together the tomato purée, demerara sugar, sherry, soy sauce, ground ginger and water in a jug then pour the sauce over the herrings.
3. Cover the casserole dish and cook on the low rack on combination 200°C/MEDIUM for 12–15 min, until the herrings are just cooked and offer no resistance to a knife when tested.
4. Serve immediately with freshly cooked vegetables or a green salad.

Buckwheat pilaf

(serves 6)

MICROWAVE: HIGH (100%)
COMBINATION: 180°C/MEDIUM (50%)

Buckwheat is quite an expensive grain, but makes a very pleasant change from rice. It is used in a lot of Russian and Eastern European peasant cookery

50g/2oz almonds
40g/1½oz butter or margarine
1 large onion, finely sliced
1 clove garlic, crushed
1×15ml/tbsp ground coriander
75g/3oz seedless raisins
450g/1lb buckwheat groats
550ml/1pt boiling vegetable stock
salt and pepper

for garnish: freshly chopped coriander

1 Place the almonds on a microwave plastic plate and cook on microwave HIGH for 3–4 min, until browned. Stir once or twice during cooking. Cool slightly and then chop roughly.
2 Place the butter in a suitable casserole dish and heat for 1–2 min on microwave HIGH. Add the onion, garlic and coriander and cook, covered, for 2–3 min.
3 Add the raisins, buckwheat and stock to the dish with most of the almonds. Cover and cook for 20 min on the low rack on combination 180°C/MEDIUM.
4 Season the pilaf to taste with salt and pepper then sprinkle with the remaining chopped almonds and plenty of freshly chopped coriander.

Aduki beans with oranges and chicory

(serves 3–4)

MICROWAVE: HIGH (100%)
COMBINATION: 180°C/MEDIUM (50%)

Aduki beans have a sweet, nutty flavour. They combine particularly well with orange

225g/8oz aduki beans
boiling water
1×15ml/tbsp oil
1 large onion, finely sliced
1 clove garlic, crushed
2 large oranges
2 bay leaves
salt and pepper
550ml/1pt boiling vegetable stock
225g/8oz chicory, trimmed and cut into halves lengthways
few drops lemon juice
1–2×15ml/tbsp demerara sugar

for garnish: chopped parsley

1 Place the aduki beans in a bowl and cover with boiling water. Cover the bowl and heat on microwave HIGH for 10 min, then allow to stand for 1 hr. Drain and rinse the beans in fresh water.
2 Heat the oil in a casserole dish for 1 min, add the onion and garlic and cook, covered, for 2–3 min on microwave HIGH. Add the drained beans.
3 Grate the rind from the oranges and add it to the beans. Peel the oranges, then chop the flesh. Add to the casserole with the bay leaves, seasonings and stock.
4 Cover the dish and cook for 20 min on the low rack on combination 180°C/MEDIUM. Remove the lid and cook for a further 10 min to reduce the liquid in the casserole slightly.
5 Sprinkle the cut chicory with the lemon juice to prevent browning then add it to the casserole. Cook, covered, for 12–15 min, until the chicory is just tender.
6 Remove the chicory from the casserole. Season the bean mixture, adding demerara sugar to taste.
7 Arrange the aduki beans in a serving dish and garnish with the chicory and plenty of freshly chopped parsley.

Left: Barbecued Pork Fillet (page 72) centre: Smoked Salmon and Prawn Quiche (page 73); right: Beef Italienne with Gnocchi (pages 73 & 93)

Main courses for special occasions

Main courses for special occasions

Fillet of beef en croûte

(serves 8) colour on title page

COMBINATION: 200°C/MEDIUM (50%) or 200°C/LOW (30%)

The perfect dish for a very special occasion. The cooking may be varied according to your preference for steak – cook on combination LOW *for a rare result, or combination* MEDIUM *for medium to well done*

3×15ml/tbsp oil
1×1.3kg/3lb fillet of beef
450g/1lb prepared puff pastry
225g/8oz mushroom pâté
1×15ml/tbsp semolina (optional)
1 egg, beaten

1. Heat the oil in a large frying pan then quickly brown the fillet on all sides. It may be necessary to have one end of the fillet hanging over the edge of the pan while browning the other end! Set to one side.
2. Roll out the pastry into a rectangle, just large enough to completely enclose the beef.
3. Beat the pâté until soft, then spread over the centre of the pastry.
4. Place the beef in the centre of the pastry, then sprinkle the top of the meat with the semolina, if used.
5. Brush the edges of the pastry with beaten egg then enclose the beef in the pastry. Invert the fillet onto a suitable baking sheet or ovenproof plate.
6. Brush the pastry with beaten egg and use any pastry trimmings to make leaves for decoration. Place the leaves on the fillet then brush again with beaten egg.
7. Cook for 23–26 min on combination 200°C/ MEDIUM or LOW, according to your preference for rare or medium to well-done steak.
8. Slice and serve with freshly cooked vegetables and potatoes.

Cook's note: *Sprinkling the pastry at the base of any dish cooked 'en croûte' with semolina will prevent the pastry becoming soggy during cooking. The semolina is not discernible in the completed dish*

Barbecued pork fillet

(serves 4–6) colour page 70

MICROWAVE: HIGH (100%)
COMBINATION: 180°C/LOW (30%) and 180°C/HIGH (100%)

5×15ml/tbsp oil
2×15ml/tbsp soy sauce
1×15ml/tbsp worcestershire sauce
2×15ml/tbsp tomato purée
2×15ml/tbsp fruit chutney
1×15ml/tbsp honey
1×5ml/tsp grained mustard
salt and freshly ground black pepper
675–900g/1½–2lb pork fillet
1 large onion, finely chopped
100ml/4fl oz stock
3 large tomatoes, skinned, deseeded and sliced

for garnish: chopped parsley

1. Place 2×15ml/tbsp of the oil into a large bowl with the soy sauce, worcestershire sauce, tomato purée, chutney, honey, mustard and salt and pepper to taste.
2. Cut the pork into 5cm/2in pieces and add to the bowl. Stir well so that the pork is coated and leave to marinade for at least 1 hr.
3. Add 2×15ml/tbsp oil to a large shallow casserole dish, stir in the onion, cover and cook in the microwave on HIGH for 4 min. Stir in the stock.
4. Add the pork to the casserole dish, arranging it in a single layer. Cook, uncovered on combination 180°C/LOW for 25–30 min until tender, gently stirring once throughout.
5. Remove the pork to a serving dish and keep hot. If necessary, boil up the sauce on combination 180°/HIGH for 5–10 min to reduce it to a syrupy consistency. Adjust the seasoning and pour the sauce over the pork.
6. Brush the tomato slices with the rest of the oil and cook in the microwave for 2–3 min until hot. Arrange them over the pork and sprinkle with parsley before serving with rice and a green salad.

Beef italienne with gnocchi

(serves 8) colour page 70

MICROWAVE: HIGH (100%)
COMBINATION: 200°C/LOW (30%)

1 quantity gnocchi romana (page 93)
2×15ml/tbsp olive oil
100g/4oz carrot, thickly sliced
1 onion, thickly sliced
1 stick celery, thickly sliced
100g/4oz cooked sliced ham, cut into strips
150ml/¼pt red wine, approximately
150ml/¼pt beef stock, approximately
2×15ml/tbsp tomato purée
bouquet garni
salt and freshly ground black pepper
1.8kg/4lb joint topside (choose a long thin joint, about 7.5–9cm/3–3½in in diameter)
15g/½oz flour, approximately
100g/4oz button mushrooms, sliced

for garnish: chopped fresh parsley or herbs

1 Prepare the gnocchi romana (steps 1–4 page 93) and leave to cool.
2 Place the oil, carrot, onion, celery and 50g/2oz of the ham into a large, shallow, covered casserole dish, stir well and cook on microwave HIGH for 5 min. Add the wine, stock, tomato purée, bouquet garni and salt and pepper to taste.
3 Wipe and weigh the joint, sprinkle with freshly ground black pepper and place on top of the vegetables in the dish with the fat side uppermost. Cook, covered, on combination 200°C/LOW allowing about 20 min per ½kg/1lb for a medium result. The centre of the joint should be at 70°C when measured with a meat thermometer.
4 Meanwhile, finish preparing the gnocchi ready for the final browning.
5 Remove the beef from the dish and keep hot. Remove the bouquet garni and then tip off as much fat from the dish as possible. Purée the juices with the vegetables and ham, and add the flour to the sauce while puréeing. If the sauce is too thick, add a little more wine or stock; if too thin, add a little extra flour.
6 Stir the mushrooms and remaining ham into the sauce then cook on microwave HIGH for 4–5 min until thickened, and the mushrooms are just soft, stirring once throughout. Keep hot.
7 Finish and brown the gnocchi.
8 Place the joint onto a hot serving dish either whole or in slices. Spoon over the sauce or keep some for handing separately. Sprinkle generously with chopped fresh parsley or herbs and serve with the gnocchi romana.

Smoked salmon and prawn quiche

(serves 8–10) colour page 71

COMBINATION: 180°C/MEDIUM (50%) and 160°C/LOW (30%)

A delicious and economical way of using smoked salmon and prawns, this quiche can also be served as a starter

for the pastry:
275g/10oz plain white flour
175g/6oz butter or margarine, softened
1 egg

for the filling:
200–225g/7–8oz smoked salmon, thinly sliced (or use smoked salmon pieces and trimmings)
100g/4oz peeled prawns
few drops lemon juice to taste
freshly ground black pepper
4 eggs
150ml/¼pt milk
salt
275ml/½pt double cream
1–2×15ml/tbsp chopped chives, optional

1 Using a mixer or food processor, work together the ingredients for the pastry to form a dough. Knead lightly and chill for 15 min.
2 Roll out on a floured surface and use to line a 28cm/11in flan dish. Prick the base well with a fork and bake blind for 10 min on combination 180°C/MEDIUM. Leave to cool slightly.
3 Arrange the thinly sliced salmon in the base of the flan case and scatter the prawns over the top. Sprinkle with a little lemon juice to taste and freshly ground black pepper.
4 Lightly beat the eggs with the milk, salt and pepper, and stir in the double cream until well blended. Pour the mixture into the flan case over the prawns and salmon. Sprinkle with chopped chives if liked.
5 Place on the low or recommended rack and cook on combination 160°C/LOW for about 30 min until the filling is set and lightly golden brown. Serve warm or cold with new potatoes and a salad.

Duck with apricots

(serves 4)

MICROWAVE: HIGH (100%)
COMBINATION: 180°C/MEDIUM (50%)

The sharp tang of fresh apricots compliments the richness of the duck and is an alternative garnish and flavouring to the more usual oranges or cherries. Ready-to-eat dried or canned apricots may be used instead

1 duck, weighing about 2½kg/5lb
salt and freshly ground black pepper
450g/1lb fresh apricots, halved and stoned
275ml/½pt stock
½ orange, juice
1×15ml/tbsp apricot brandy or cointreau, optional
2×15ml/tbsp brandy, optional

1. Wipe the prepared duck with a damp cloth. Prick the skin well, sprinkle with a little salt and pepper and rub it into the skin.
2. Arrange the duck on the low or recommended rack over the drip tray and splatter guard (where provided) and roast on combination 180°C/MEDIUM allowing a total of 10–12 min per ½kg/1lb.
3. Twelve minutes before the end of the cooking time, arrange half the apricots on the splatter guard or on a plate under the duck and continue cooking.
4. Remove the duck and place onto a hot serving plate or dish and keep warm. Pour off most of the fat and juices from the pan reserving 3–4× 15ml/tbsp of the juices.
5. Deglaze the pan with the stock. Place the stock and duck juices into a bowl or dish and cook on combination for 8–10 min until slightly reduced and syrupy.
6. Allow the liquid to cool slightly then purée with the orange juice and cooked apricots. Adjust the seasoning to taste.
7. Meanwhile, heat the remaining apricots in the microwave on HIGH until warm, about 2 min. If desired, heat the liqueur and brandy for 1 min until bubbling, pour over the duck and ignite. Do not ignite in the oven.
8. Arrange the apricots around the duck and serve straight away with the apricot sauce handed separately.

Cook's note: *For more crispy skin, at the end of the roasting time remove the apricots and cook the duck on convection only at 250°C for 5 min*

Dorset fish cobbler

(serves 4–6)

MICROWAVE: HIGH (100%)
COMBINATION: 200°C/LOW (30%)

40g/1½oz butter
1 onion, finely chopped
175g/6oz mushrooms, sliced
1 cooking apple, diced
40g/1½oz flour
275ml/½pt cider
450g/1lb haddock, cut into large cubes
salt and pepper
1×5ml/tsp dried mixed herbs
225g/8oz peeled prawns
3–4×15ml/tbsp cream, optional

for the cobbler topping:
100g/4oz self-raising flour
100g/4oz self-raising wholewheat flour
50g/2oz butter
75–150ml/3–5fl oz soured cream or milk
1 medium-size cooking apple, grated
milk to glaze

1. In a large covered casserole dish, melt the butter on microwave HIGH for 1 min, stir in the onion, cover and cook for 4 min. Stir in the mushrooms and apple and continue to cook for 4–6 min until tender, stirring once or twice.
2. Blend in the flour, add the cider and cook for a further 3–4 min until thickened and boiling. Add the haddock, seasoning, herbs, prawns and cream. Cover and cook on combination 200°C/LOW for 10–14 min.
3. Meanwhile make the cobbler topping. Place the flours into a bowl, rub in the butter and add sufficient cream or milk to form a dough. Roll out into a 25cm/10in square.
4. Spread the grated apple over the dough then roll up like a swiss roll, dampening the edge with a little milk to seal. Cut the roll into 12 slices.
5. Remove the hot casserole dish from the oven and arrange the pinwheel scones around the outside edge, overlapping them slightly. Brush the scones with milk.
6. Continue to cook on combination for 8–10 min or until the scones are well risen and lightly golden. Sprinkle with chopped parsley.

Scallops with Asparagus (page 24); Spiced Herrings with Pepper (page 68)

Pork with fresh herbs

(serves 6)

MICROWAVE: HIGH (100%)
COMBINATION: 160°C/LOW (30%) and 200°C/HIGH (100%)

This delicious pork casserole makes a welcome change from the more usual beef casseroles for any special occasion. Serve with fresh vegetables and baked potatoes (page 92)

2×15ml/tbsp olive oil
1 large onion, finely sliced
1 large carrot, peeled and cut into matchsticks
1 stick celery, sliced
100g/4oz unsmoked streaky bacon, rinded and chopped
1.4kg/3lb boneless shoulder pork, crackling removed and reserved
2×15ml/tbsp wholewheat flour
salt and pepper
2×15ml/tbsp freshly chopped mixed herbs
1 bay leaf
275ml/10fl oz white wine or stock
150ml/5fl oz soured cream

for garnish: freshly chopped herbs

1 Heat the oil in a suitable large casserole dish for 2 min on microwave HIGH, add the prepared vegetables and cook, covered, for 6–8 min. Stir once during cooking.
2 Add the bacon and cook for a further 2 min.
3 Cut the pork into small cubes and toss in the flour. Add to the casserole and cook for 6–8 min, stirring once.
4 Season the pork with salt and pepper and add the herbs and bay leaf. Add the wine or stock then cover the casserole.
5 Cook on combination 160°C/LOW for 1hr, or until the pork is tender. Remove the casserole from the oven.
6 Score the crackling deeply then cook for 8–10 min on combination 200°C/HIGH. Chop roughly.
7 Reheat the casserole for 4–5 min on microwave HIGH if necessary. Remove the bay leaf and season to taste. Stir in the soured cream, then scatter the chopped crackling over the casserole and garnish with freshly chopped herbs before serving.

Cook's note: *Break the bay leaf in half before adding to the casserole. This will allow more flavour to be released from the leaf during cooking*

Salmon tourtière

(serves 8–10)

MICROWAVE: MEDIUM (50%)
COMBINATION: 180°C/LOW (30%)

for the pastry:
275g/10oz plain flour
pinch salt
175g/6oz butter
1 egg

for the filling:
50g/2oz cracked wheat
15g/½oz butter, softened
2 eggs
225g/8oz fresh haddock, finely chopped
8–10 spring onions, finely sliced
salt, pepper and cayenne
1–2 eggs, beaten
450g/1lb fresh salmon, cut into cubes
1 lemon, finely sliced

for serving: soured cream

1. Make the pastry by blending all the ingredients to form a firm dough. Knead lightly and leave to chill for 1 hr.
2. Place the cracked wheat into a bowl, pour on enough cold water to cover then leave to soak for 30 min. Drain thoroughly, squeezing out as much water as possible.
3. Use a little butter to grease 2 small dishes, cups or ramekins. Break an egg into each dish, prick the yolks and dot with the remaining butter.
4. Cover the eggs and cook on microwave MEDIUM for 2½–3½ min until set firmly. Leave to cool then chop finely.
5. Place the haddock into a large mixing bowl with the spring onions, cracked wheat and chopped eggs. Add salt, pepper and cayenne to taste and bind the mixture with a little beaten egg.
6. Roll out two-thirds of the pastry and line a 20cm/8in microwave cake dish with removable base. (Alternatively, use a dish of similar diameter with a depth of about 5cm/2in, and line with baking parchment or greaseproof, leaving two or three 'handles' at the top to make removal of the cooked pie from the dish easier.)
7. Place half the haddock mixture into the base of the pastry-lined dish, arrange the salmon over the top and cover with the rest of the haddock mixture. Place the lemon slices over the top.
8. Roll out the rest of the pastry, cover the pie and dampen, seal and flute the edges. Make a small slit or hole in the top centre of the pie and use the trimmings of pastry to cut small shapes or leaves to decorate.
9. Brush the top of the pie with beaten egg and cook on combination 180°C/LOW for 30–40 min until light golden brown. (If preferred, for the last 5–10 min of cooking, the pie may be removed from the dish, brushed all over with beaten egg and then placed on a baking plate to finish cooking.)
10. Serve hot, warm or cold with soured cream.

Swiss turkey

(serves 6)

COMBINATION: 200°C/MEDIUM (50%)

675g/1½lb turkey breast fillet
salt and freshly ground black pepper
75g/3oz butter, melted
350–450g/¾–1lb cooked spinach, chopped
grated nutmeg
6 slices cooked ham
175g/6oz gruyère or emmental cheese, thinly sliced
1 wineglass dry white wine
150ml/¼pt turkey or chicken stock, approximately

for serving: noodles or french bread, and a green salad

1. Place the turkey fillet under baking parchment or greaseproof and beat flat with a rolling pin.
2. Cut into 6 pieces and sprinkle with salt and pepper. Brush with some of the melted butter and arrange in a single layer in a large casserole dish. Cook for 8–10 min on combination 200°C/MEDIUM.
3. Drain the spinach very well, squeezing as much liquid from it as possible. Beat in salt and nutmeg to taste and a little melted butter.
4. Remove the turkey from the cooking dish and pour the juices into a measuring jug. Clean the dish and brush with the remaining butter.
5. Cut the ham slices in half and place half of them in the base of the cooking dish. Arrange the spinach over the ham and top with the turkey. Cover with the rest of the ham and the cheese slices.
6. Add the wine to the jug with the juices and make up to 275ml/½pt with stock. Pour into the dish. Cook for 15–18 min until golden. Serve straight from the dish with noodles or french bread, and a green salad.

Carbonnades à la flamande

(serves 6)

MICROWAVE: HIGH (100%), optional
COMBINATION: 200°C/HIGH (100%), 160°C/LOW (30%) and 200°C/MEDIUM (50%)

3×15ml/tbsp olive oil
25g/1oz unsalted butter
3 large onions, sliced
1¼–1½kg/2½–3lb braising steak, trimmed and cut into 2.5cm/1in cubes
3–4 cloves garlic, crushed or finely chopped, optional
salt and freshly ground black pepper
2×15ml/tbsp flour
1×15ml/tbsp brown sugar
425ml/¾pt brown ale
1×15ml/tbsp wine vinegar
150–275ml/¼–½pt boiling beef stock
1 bouquet garni
2 bay leaves

for the garlic crust:
3 cloves garlic, crushed
175–225g/6–8oz unsalted butter, melted
12×15mm/½in slices french bread

1 Place the olive oil and the butter into a large, shallow casserole dish. Stir in the onions, cover and cook on combination 200°C/HIGH or microwave HIGH for 8–10 min until softened, stirring once throughout.
2 Add the steak, mix well and continue to cook, covered, for 10–12 min, stirring once.
3 Add the garlic if used, seasoning and flour, mix well then stir in the brown sugar, brown ale, wine vinegar and sufficient beef stock to just cover the meat. Add the bouquet garni and bay leaves to the dish.
4 Cover and cook on combination 200°C/HIGH or microwave HIGH for about 8–10 min or until boiling, stirring once. Change to combination 160°C/LOW and continue to cook for about 1½ hr or until the meat is tender. If preferred, remove the bouquet garni and bay leaves from the dish. Adjust the seasoning to taste.
5 If the carbonnades has produced too much gravy, spoon some from the dish into a sauce jug and reserve, leaving the carbonnades so that the meat is just covered. Wipe around the top edges of the dish if necessary.
6 For the garlic crust topping, stir the crushed garlic into the melted butter and dip in the french bread slices so they are well coated and have absorbed some of the butter.
7 Arrange the bread on top of the carbonnades in a single layer. Cook, uncovered, on combination 200°C/MEDIUM for 9–11 min or until the garlic crust is crisp with a golden tinge. Serve straight from the dish with any reserved gravy handed separately.

Lamb kebabs with juniper

(serves 4) colour opposite

COMBINATION: 200°C/LOW (30%)

550g/1¼lb boned leg or shoulder of lamb
freshly ground black pepper
100g/4oz bacon
1 clove garlic
6 juniper berries
4 slices stale bread, crusts removed
sage leaves
2 slices raw gammon, 1cm/½in thick, cut into cubes
oil for brushing

1 Cut the lamb into 2.5-4cm/1–1½in cubes and sprinkle with freshly ground black pepper.
2 Chop the bacon, garlic and juniper berries finely, or grind in a food processor or blender. Cut each slice of bread into 4 squares and spread with the bacon mixture.
3 Thread the lamb, seasoned bread, sage leaves and gammon onto either 4×25cm/10in or 8×12.5cm/5in skewers, placing the bread with the seasoned side facing the lamb and alternating the ingredients until they are all used.
4 Brush the kebabs liberally with oil and place onto the recommended rack, ensuring that skewers, if metal, are not touching the metal rack or the interior surface of the oven.
5 Cook for 22–25 min on combination 200°C/LOW, turning the kebabs over halfway through. Remove from the oven when the meat is browned but before the bread is too crisp. Serve hot with rice and a salad.

Crab and Avocado Cheesecake (page 25); Lamb Kebabs with Juniper (above)

Mackerel calaisienne

(serves 4)

MICROWAVE: HIGH (100%) and MEDIUM (50%)
COMBINATION: 180°C/MEDIUM (50%)

for the mustard sauce:
25g/1oz butter
25g/1oz flour
225ml/8fl oz chicken stock
75ml/2½fl oz top of the milk or half cream
salt and freshly ground black pepper
squeeze lemon juice
1×5ml/tsp dijon mustard

for the mackerel:
50g/2oz butter, approximately
1 small onion, finely chopped
2 eggs
50–75g/2–3oz bread, soaked in a little milk
1 clove garlic, crushed
½ lemon, grated rind
2×5ml/tsp each finely chopped fresh thyme and parsley
½×5ml/tsp anchovy paste or purée
salt and freshly ground black pepper
2 large mackerel, weighing about 550–675g/1¼–1½lb each, filleted

for garnish: fresh chopped parsley

1. Place the butter for the sauce into a bowl and melt for 1 min on microwave HIGH and blend in the flour. Add the stock gradually and cook for 3–4 min until thickened and boiling, whisking well 2–3 times throughout.
2. Stir in the top of the milk or half cream and seasoning then cook on microwave MEDIUM for 3 min, stirring 2–3 times. Beat in the lemon juice and mustard. Set the sauce to one side.
3. Prepare the stuffing for the mackerel. In a bowl or dish, melt 15g/½oz butter on microwave HIGH for 20–30 sec, stir in the onion, cover and cook for 3 min. Leave to cool.
4. Place 6g/¼oz butter into each of 2 small dishes, cups or ramekins and melt on microwave HIGH for 20–30 sec. Break an egg into each dish, prick the yolks, cover and cook on MEDIUM for 2½–3 min until whites and yolks are firmly set. Leave to cool then chop.
5. Squeeze most of the milk from the bread, chop and add to the cooled onions with the chopped eggs, garlic, lemon, herbs, anchovy paste and seasoning. Mix well together.
6. Remove any roes from the fish, chop and mix into the stuffing. Trim away any fins from the mackerel fillets, then wash and dry. Spread the stuffing over the 4 fillets and roll up from the tail end. Arrange in a buttered dish then dot with slivers of the remaining butter.
7. Cover with greaseproof paper and cook on combination 180°C/MEDIUM for 20–25 min. Keep hot while reheating the sauce on microwave MEDIUM for 3–4 min, beating well twice throughout.
8. Pour the mustard sauce onto a hot serving dish and arrange the mackerel on the top. Sprinkle with plenty of chopped parsley and serve straight away.

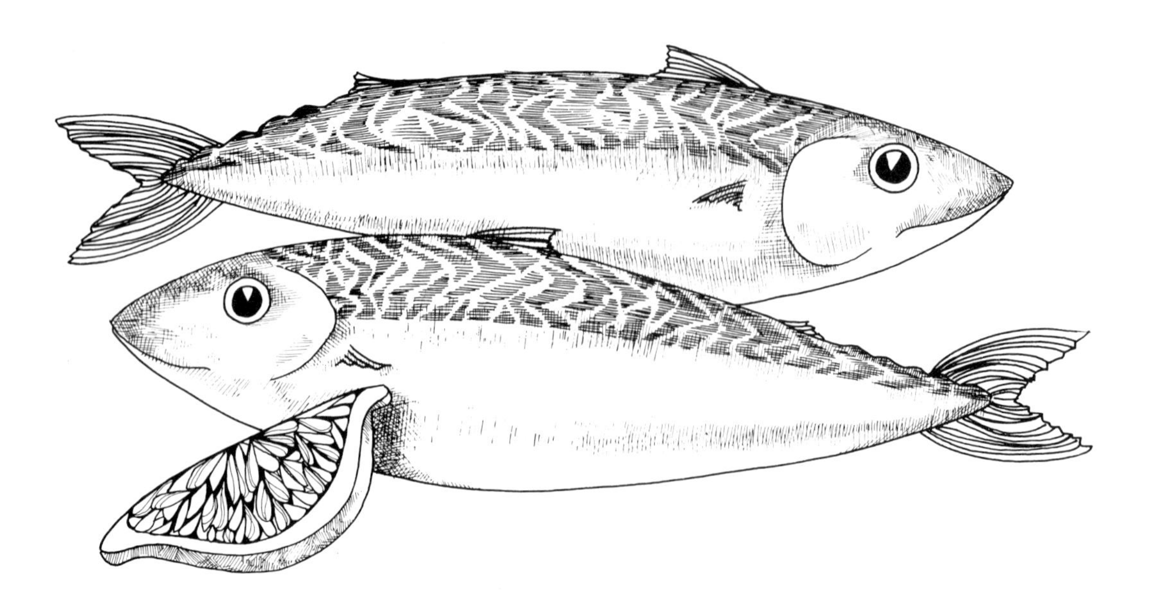

Lemon and thyme chickens with golden stuffing

(serves 8)

MICROWAVE: HIGH (100%)
COMBINATION: 200°C/MEDIUM (50%) and 180°C/MEDIUM (50%)

for the stuffing:
175g/6oz carrots, grated
225g/8oz onion, grated
450g/1lb pork sausage meat
350g/12oz fresh brown breadcrumbs
1×15ml/tbsp chopped fresh thyme or 1×5ml/tsp dried thyme
salt and pepper
beaten egg to bind
slivers butter or margarine

for the chickens:
2×1.1–1.2kg/2½–2¾lb chickens
salt and pepper
1 onion, quartered
melted butter or margarine for brushing

for the sauce:
425ml/¾pt chicken stock, approximately
3×15ml/tbsp cornflour
1 lemon, grated rind and juice
2×15ml/tbsp chopped fresh thyme or 2×5ml/tsp dried thyme
150ml/¼pt soured cream

for garnish: watercress

1. Combine all the ingredients for the stuffing except the slivers of butter, mixing well together. Either form into balls, or spoon into a large shallow dish. Top with slivers of butter or margarine and cook on combination 200°C/MEDIUM for about 20 min until light golden brown and cooked through. Set to one side.
2. Wipe the chickens inside and out with a damp cloth. Season the cavities and place some onion in each. Brush all over with melted butter and place into a large covered dish. If you do not have a dish large enough, use a large roasting bag and secure loosely with string. Place the dish on the low or recommended rack or, if turntable or oven shelf. Cook on combination 180°C/MEDIUM allowing 9–10 min per ½kg/1lb.
3. Test the chickens with a skewer inserted into the thigh – the juices should run clear. Keep the chickens warm on a serving platter.
4. Skim off the fat from the juices. Place the juices into a measuring jug and make up to 675ml/1¼pt with the chicken stock. Blend the cornflour with a little of the stock then add the remainder.
5. Cook on microwave HIGH for 5–6 min until thickened and boiling, stirring well once or twice throughout. Add the lemon rind and juice, the thyme, salt and pepper to taste and finally stir in the soured cream.
6. Reheat the stuffing for 6–7 min on combination 200°C/MEDIUM then reheat the sauce for 2–3 min on microwave HIGH.
7. Pour a little of the sauce around or over the chickens and garnish the dish with watercress and stuffing balls if made, otherwise hand the dish of stuffing separately.

Chicken kiev

(serves 4)

COMBINATION: 200°C/LOW (30%)

This oven-baked version of the classic dish which is normally deep-fat fried will help save a few calories for the diet conscious

50g/2oz butter
2 cloves garlic, crushed
4 chicken breasts, skinned and boned
1 egg, beaten
75–100g/3–4oz dried breadcrumbs
oil or melted butter for brushing

for garnish: parsley sprigs

1. Beat the butter with the crushed garlic to make a garlic butter. Cover and leave to harden in the fridge for 20–30 min.
2. Make a slit in each chicken breast and insert a 15g/½oz portion of garlic butter into each pocket.
3. Dip each breast in beaten egg then coat thoroughly in breadcrumbs. Chill for 1–2 hr in the fridge.
4. Thoroughly brush a dish with oil or melted butter and add the chicken in a single layer. Drizzle the tops and sides of the chicken breasts with the rest of the oil or butter.
5. Place the dish on the low or recommended rack and bake for 20–25 min on combination 200°C/LOW, turning the chicken over halfway through. Serve hot garnished with parsley sprigs.

Veal with normandy sauce

(serves 6)

MICROWAVE: HIGH (100%)
COMBINATION: 200°C/MEDIUM (50%)

6 veal chops or cutlets, weighing about 175g/6oz each
3×15ml/tbsp olive oil
few drops lemon juice
freshly ground black pepper
225g/8oz button mushrooms, sliced

for the sauce:
25g/1oz unsalted butter
1 onion, finely chopped
25g/1oz plain flour
175ml/6fl oz chicken stock
1 wineglass dry white wine
salt and freshly ground black pepper
¼×5ml/tsp grated nutmeg
4×15ml/tbsp double cream
1×5ml/tsp lemon juice

for garnish: watercress
for serving: freshly cooked pasta and flageolets

1. Brush the veal with 1×15ml/tbsp of the oil, sprinkle with lemon juice and black pepper. Place the veal on the low or recommended rack over the drip tray and splatter guard (if fitted) and cook on combination 200°C/MEDIUM for 15–18 min until the meat is tender and no longer pink. Toss the mushrooms in the remaining oil and place on the drip tray under the veal halfway through the cooking time.
2. Lift the veal and arrange on a hot serving platter and scatter the mushrooms over the top. Keep hot, and reserve the meat juices.
3. For the sauce, melt the butter in a bowl or jug in the microwave on HIGH for 1 min. Stir in the onion, cover and cook for 5 min.
4. Stir in the flour, add the stock gradually then stir in the reserved juices, wine, seasoning and nutmeg. Cook in the microwave on HIGH for 3–4 min until thickened and boiling, whisking every minute.
5. Stir the double cream into the sauce with the lemon juice and adjust the seasoning. Spoon some of the sauce over the veal and mushrooms.
6. Arrange the pasta and flageolets around the veal and garnish with watercress before serving hot. Hand the rest of the sauce separately.

Cook's note: *Pork or lamb chops can be used instead of veal*

Rack of lamb with cumberland sauce

(serves 2) colour opposite

MICROWAVE: HIGH (100%) and MEDIUM (50%)
COMBINATION: 180°C/LOW (30%)

for the sauce:
1 orange
150ml/¼pt boiling water
4×15ml/tbsp redcurrant jelly
½ lemon, juice
1 liqueur glass port wine

for the rack of lamb:
1 best end of neck, chined and barked
oil for brushing

for decoration: cutlet frills
for serving: jardinière platter (page 93)

1. Thinly pare the rind from a quarter of the orange cut it into thin shreds, and place into a bowl. Add the water, cover and cook in the microwave on HIGH for 1–2 min until boiling then on MEDIUM for 5 min until tender. Drain and rinse well.
2. Squeeze and strain the juice from the orange. Heat the redcurrant jelly on HIGH for 2 min then whisk in the strained orange juice, the lemon juice and port. Leave until cold and stir in the orange rind.
3. Cut away the main bone and trim the meat from cutlet bones back about 1.5cm/½in to expose the ends of the bones. Weigh the joint, then shield the bone tips and the ends of the joint with small, smooth pieces of aluminium foil. Brush the joint with oil.
4. Place the joint with the fat side uppermost, either on a trivet in a dish, or directly on the low or recommended rack over the drip tray and splatter guard, but the foil must not be allowed to touch the rack, or the interior oven walls.
5. Cook on combination 180°C/LOW, allowing 17–20 min per ½kg/1lb for a medium to well-done result. Remove the foil and place the joint onto a hot serving dish.
6. Place a cutlet frill on each bone tip and serve with the cold cumberland sauce and a jardinière platter.

Rack of Lamb with Cumberland Sauce (above); Jardinière Platter (page 93)

Chicken gruyère
(serves 4)

MICROWAVE: HIGH (100%)
COMBINATION: 200°C/MEDIUM (50%)

4 chicken breasts, skinned and boned
150g/5oz gruyère cheese, cut into 4 fingers
freshly ground black pepper
8 rashers streaky bacon, derinded
150ml/¼pt chicken stock
5×15ml/tbsp double cream
2 egg yolks
½×5ml/tsp dried dill
salt

1. Remove the loose fillet from the underneath of each chicken breast. Arrange the breasts and fillets on a board, cover with baking parchment and beat with a rolling pin to flatten.
2. Replace the fillets onto the breasts, place a piece of cheese onto each one and roll up into parcels. Sprinkle with black pepper.
3. Cut the rashers in halves lengthwise, wrap the strips around the chicken parcels diagonally and tuck underneath or secure with wooden cocktail sticks.
4. Place the parcels into a shallow dish and add the chicken stock. Cover and cook on combination 200°C/MEDIUM for 10 min, then remove the lid and cook for a further 10–15 min.
5. Remove the chicken and any melted cheese to a hot serving dish. Keep warm.
6. Whisk together the cream, egg yolks and dill, and beat into the hot stock. Cook on microwave HIGH for 2–3 min until thickened. Do not allow to boil and whisk every 30 sec. Adjust seasoning with salt and pepper.
7. Pour a little of the sauce around the chicken and hand the rest separately.

Veal with stilton and cream sauce
(serves 4)

MICROWAVE: HIGH (100%)
COMBINATION: 200°C/MEDIUM (50%)

50g/2oz butter
4×150–175g/5–6oz veal steaks
few drops lemon juice
freshly ground black pepper
40g/1½oz stilton cheese
1×15ml/tbsp brandy
2×15ml/tbsp dry white wine
225ml/8fl oz double cream

1. Melt 15g/½oz of the butter in the microwave on HIGH for 25–30 sec in a large shallow dish. Add the veal steaks in a single layer and brush with the butter.
2. Sprinkle with a few drops of lemon juice and freshly ground black pepper. Place on the low or recommended rack and cook on combination 200°C/MEDIUM for 10 min.
3. Meanwhile, mash the stilton with a fork. Add the remaining butter and beat until creamy. Beat in the brandy and black pepper to taste.
4. Remove the veal steaks and arrange them in a single layer in a hot ovenproof serving dish. Keep warm.
5. Stir the wine into the cooking dish and boil for 5–8 min on combination until slightly reduced. Stir in the cream.
6. Pour the cream sauce over the veal and cook on combination for 5 min. Place spoonfuls of the stilton mixture onto each veal steak and continue to cook for 2–3 min until the cheese has melted.
7. Serve with plain noodles or rice.

Turkey and ham gougère
(serves 4–6)

MICROWAVE: HIGH (100%)
COMBINATION: 200°C/LOW (30%)

25g/1oz butter or margarine
1 small onion, chopped
1 stick celery, thinly sliced
½ green or red pepper, deseeded and diced
1×5ml/tsp finely chopped tarragon
1×15ml/tbsp flour
150ml/¼pt chicken stock
225g/8oz cooked turkey, diced
50g/2oz cooked ham, diced
2–3×15ml/tbsp natural yogurt or cream
salt and freshly ground black pepper
1×15ml/tbsp parmesan cheese

for the choux pastry:
150ml/¼pt water
50g/2oz butter or margarine
65g/2½oz plain flour
pinch salt
2 eggs, beaten
50g/2oz cheddar cheese, finely grated

1. Lightly oil a 1½ litre/2½pt shallow oval or round dish.
2. Melt the butter or margarine in a bowl or dish

for 1 min on microwave HIGH. Stir in the onion, celery and pepper. Cover and cook for 3 min.

3 Add the tarragon and flour and stir well. Stir in the stock. Cook in the microwave for 2–3 min until thickened and boiling, stirring once halfway through.

4 Stir in the turkey, ham and natural yogurt or cream. Add salt and freshly ground black pepper to taste.

5 For the choux pastry, place the water and butter or margarine into a mixing bowl and heat in the microwave for 2–3 min on HIGH until melted and boiling rapidly.

6 Add the flour and salt all at once then beat thoroughly until thickened and smooth. Beat in the eggs a little at a time, and finally beat in the cheese. The mixture should be glossy and sufficiently thick to hold its shape.

7 Arrange spoonfuls of the choux pastry around the edges of the prepared dish without spreading it across the base. Spoon the filling into the centre and smooth down.

8 Sprinkle with the parmesan cheese and place on the low or recommended rack. Cook on combination 200°C/LOW for 25–28 min, until well risen and golden brown.

9 Serve within a few minutes. A tossed salad goes well with this dish, perhaps with a few plain boiled new potatoes.

Red mullet en papillote

(serves 4)

COMBINATION: 200°C/MEDIUM (50%)

4 red mullet, weighing 200–225g/7–8oz each, cleaned
50–65g/2–2½oz butter, softened
salt and freshly ground black pepper
lemon juice for sprinkling

for serving: melted butter and lemon wedges

1 Cut an oval of greaseproof paper for each fish, large enough to enclose it and allowing a little extra to fold and crimp the edges.

2 Spread the centres of the greaseproof papers with the softened butter and place a fish on each one. Sprinkle with seasoning and lemon juice.

3 Fold the papers edge-to-edge to enclose the fish. Fold over a double 'seam' at the edges, press well then crimp in a concertina form to prevent them from undoing.

4 Place the parcels on the turntable and cook for 11–14 min, rearranging the outside ones to the centre and vice versa halfway through cooking.

5 Either serve the fish in their parcels, or carefully remove them onto hot serving plates. Serve with extra melted butter and lemon wedges.

Roast pheasants with cranberry and orange sauce

(serves 4) *colour page 99*

MICROWAVE: HIGH (100%)
COMBINATION: 180°C/MEDIUM (50%)

2 pheasants, each weighing about 550g/1¼lb when prepared
melted butter
streaky bacon rashers
1×15ml/tbsp cornflour
150ml/¼pt jellied game or poultry stock
1 wineglass red wine
1 orange, grated rind and juice
175g/6oz jar cranberry sauce
salt and freshly ground black pepper
pinch grated nutmeg

for garnish: orange slices and watercress

1 Wipe the pheasants and brush each one inside and out with melted butter. Wrap in streaky bacon rashers and place on the low or recommended rack over the drip tray and splatter guard (if fitted).

2 Roast on combination 180°C/MEDIUM allowing 8–10 min per ½kg/lb. Remove the bacon from the breasts of the pheasants about 5 min before the end of cooking. Leave the pheasants to stand and keep warm.

3 Blend the cornflour with the stock and add the wine, orange rind and juice, cranberry sauce, seasoning and nutmeg. Heat in the microwave on HIGH for 4 min until thickened and boiling, stirring once or twice throughout.

4 Pour off the fat from the pheasant and bacon juices, and deglaze the pan with the sauce. Reheat if necessary for 1–2 min on HIGH.

5 Flood a hot serving dish with a little of the sauce and arrange the pheasants on the top. Alternatively, place the pheasants onto the dish and pour a little of the sauce over the top.

6 Garnish with orange slices and a little watercress and hand the rest of the sauce separately. Serve straight away.

Accompaniments and side dishes

Above: Spinach with Soured Cream and Peanuts (page 92); below left: Leeks with Chillis (page 89); centre: Jerusalem Artichokes with Peppers (page 88); right: Potatoes au Gratin (page 88)

Accompaniments and side dishes

Jerusalem artichokes with peppers

(serves 3) colour page 86

MICROWAVE: HIGH (100%)
COMBINATION: 160°C/LOW (30%)

15g/½oz butter
1×15ml/tbsp olive oil
1 small onion, finely sliced
½ red pepper, cut into strips
450g/1lb jerusalem artichokes, peeled
white pepper
salt
150ml/5fl oz single cream

1 Heat the butter and oil in a suitable casserole dish for 1 min on microwave HIGH, add the onion and cook, covered, for a further 2 min. Add the pepper strips and cook, covered, for 3 min.
2 Add the peeled artichokes to the casserole. Season the vegetables with white pepper and a little salt.
4 Cover the casserole dish and cook for 12–15 min on the low rack on combination 160°C/LOW.
5 Stir in the cream and serve immediately.

Potatoes au gratin

(serves 4–6) colour page 87

COMBINATION: 180°C/LOW (30%)

1kg/2¼lb potatoes
2–3 medium-size onions
1 clove garlic
75–100g/3–4oz butter or margarine
175–200g/6–7oz cheese, grated
salt and freshly ground black pepper
275ml/½pt double or single cream
150ml/¼pt milk or single cream, optional

1 Peel and grate the potatoes or cut them into very thin matchsticks. Rinse and drain thoroughly. Finely slice the onions.
2 Rub the clove of garlic around the inside of a large casserole dish or crush it and add to the rest of the ingredients. Use some of the butter to grease the dish well.
3 Arrange alternate layers of the potatoes, onions, slivers of butter and most of the cheese in the dish, seasoning each layer with salt and pepper and reserving a little of the butter for the top.
4 Pour over the 275ml/½pt cream, sprinkle with the rest of the cheese and top with slivers of the remaining butter.
5 Cook for 30–40 min on combination 180°C/LOW, adding a little milk or extra cream if necessary to prevent the dish becoming dry. Leave to stand for 5 min before serving with any plain meat or poultry dish.

Baked vegetable rice

(serves 4–6) colour page 43

MICROWAVE: HIGH (100%)
COMBINATION: 200°C/MEDIUM (50%)

25g/1oz ghee or butter
1 large onion, sliced
1 clove garlic, crushed
1 green chilli, finely chopped (optional)
1 small aubergine, finely diced
½ red pepper, chopped
225g/8oz brown rice
550ml/1pt boiling vegetable stock
salt and pepper

for garnish: chopped parsley or coriander

1 Heat the ghee or butter in a large casserole dish for 1–2 min on microwave HIGH. Add the onion, garlic and chilli, if used, and cook for 2 min, covered.
2 Stir the aubergine and red pepper into the dish and cook for a further 3 min, covered.
3 Stir the rice into the vegetables, then add the boiling stock. Cover and cook on the low rack on combination 200°C/MEDIUM for 30 min.
4 Allow the rice to stand for 5 min then season to taste with salt and pepper. Garnish with freshly chopped parsley or coriander and serve.

Leeks with chillis

(serves 4) colour page 86

MICROWAVE: HIGH (100%)
COMBINATION: 160°C/MEDIUM (50%)

900g/2lb leeks, trimmed, washed and sliced
salt and pepper
4×15ml/tbsp water
113g/3.9oz can green chillis in brine, drained
150ml/5fl oz single cream or natural yogurt

for garnish: watercress

1 Place the sliced leeks in a microwave dish with a pinch of salt and the water. Cover and cook for 10–12 min on microwave HIGH until soft, stirring once.
2 Place the leeks in a liquidiser or food processor with the chillis and cream or yogurt. Blend to a smooth purée and season to taste with salt and pepper.
3 Turn the purée into a serving dish and heat for 10 min on the low rack on combination 160°C/MEDIUM until hot. Garnish with watercress and serve.

Brussels sprouts with stilton and walnut sauce

(serves 4) colour page 115

MICROWAVE: HIGH (100%)
COMBINATION: 200°C/MEDIUM (50%)

This unusual way of serving brussels sprouts is a perfect accompaniment to the traditional Christmas turkey and ham

675g/1½lb brussels sprouts, trimmed and scored
3×15ml/tbsp water
25g/1oz butter or margarine
25g/1oz flour
200ml/8fl oz milk
150ml/5fl oz soured cream or natural yogurt
50g/2oz walnuts, chopped
50g/2oz stilton cheese, crumbled
salt and pepper

1 Place the brussels sprouts in a large microwave casserole dish with the water. Cover and cook for 10–12 min on microwave HIGH, until the sprouts are just cooked. Stir once during cooking. Leave the sprouts until required.
2 Heat the butter or margarine in a jug or bowl for 1–2 min on microwave HIGH. Stir in the flour then gradually add the milk. Heat for 3–4 min, stirring every minute, until boiling and thickened.
3 Add the soured cream or yogurt to the sauce with most of the walnuts and the stilton. Stir well then season to taste.
4 Combine the brussels sprouts with the sauce in an open vegetable serving dish. Sprinkle with the remaining walnuts and cook on the low rack on combination 200°C/MEDIUM for 10 min. Serve immediately.

Spiced sweet potato with almonds

(serves 4) colour page 43

MICROWAVE: HIGH (100%) and MEDIUM (50%)
COMBINATION: 180°C/MEDIUM (50%)

25g/1oz ghee or butter
50g/2oz blanched almonds
1 large onion, sliced
1 clove garlic, crushed
1×5ml/tsp turmeric
½×5ml/tsp chilli powder
1×5ml/tsp ground cumin
1×5ml/tsp concentrated hot curry paste
675g/1½lb sweet potato, peeled, sliced and cut into fingers
150ml/5fl oz boiling stock
1×15ml/tbsp tomato purée
salt and pepper
150ml/5fl oz set natural yogurt

for garnish: blanched almonds and lime butterflies

1 Heat the ghee or butter in a large dish for 1–2 min on microwave HIGH, add the almonds and cook for 4 min, stirring once, until the almonds are a pale golden brown.
2 Add the onion, garlic, turmeric, chilli, cumin and curry paste and cook, covered, for 4 min, stirring once.
3 Add the sweet potato to the dish with the stock and tomato purée. Season with salt and pepper then cook, covered, for 20 min on the low rack on combination 180°C/MEDIUM, stirring once during cooking.
4 Check the seasoning and stir in the yogurt. Heat for 2–3 min on microwave MEDIUM, if necessary, then serve, garnished with almonds and lime butterflies.

Baked peppers with sweetcorns and garlic

(serves 6) colour opposite

MICROWAVE: HIGH (100%) and MEDIUM (50%)
COMBINATION: 180°C/MEDIUM (50%)

25g/1oz butter
1×15ml/tbsp olive oil
3 large green peppers, cored and cut into 6 segments each
1 clove garlic, crushed
125g/4oz baby sweetcorns
salt and pepper
150ml/5fl oz single cream

1 Heat the butter and oil together in a shallow serving dish for 1–2 min on microwave HIGH. Add the peppers and garlic and cook, covered, for 15 min on the low rack on combination 180°C/MEDIUM.
2 Add the sweetcorns and cook for a further 5 min.
3 Season with salt and pepper and stir in the cream. Heat on microwave MEDIUM for 2–3 min to warm the cream, then serve.

Courgettes with basil and cucumber

(serves 4) colour opposite

MICROWAVE: HIGH (100%)
COMBINATION: 180°C/LOW (30%)

50g/2oz butter
450g/1lb courgettes, trimmed and sliced
½ cucumber, peeled and diced
salt and pepper
1–2×15ml/tbsp freshly chopped basil
25g/1oz chopped almonds

1 Heat the butter in a casserole dish for 1–2 min on microwave HIGH. Add the courgettes and cook, covered, for 3 min.
2 Add the cucumber, salt and pepper and most of the basil to the dish. Cover and cook for 10–15 min on the low rack on combination 180°C/LOW, until the courgettes and cucumber are tender.
3 Check the seasoning and sprinkle with the remaining basil, mixed with the almonds. Serve immediately with white meat or poultry.

Leeks au gratin

(serves 3–4) colour opposite

MICROWAVE: HIGH (100%)
COMBINATION: 200°C/LOW (30%)

450g/1lb leeks, trimmed and cut into 5–7.5cm/2–3in lengths
2×15ml/tbsp water
25g/1oz butter or margarine
25g/1oz flour
275ml/10fl oz milk
salt and pepper
75g/3oz cheddar cheese, grated

1 Soak the leeks for 10–15 min to clean any dirt from them. Place them in a microwave dish with the water and cook, covered, for 3 min on microwave HIGH. Leave to stand.
2 Prepare the cheese sauce. Melt the butter or margarine in a jug on microwave HIGH for 1–2 min, then stir in the flour. Gradually add the milk then heat for 4–5 min, stirring every minute, until the sauce is boiling and thickened. Season to taste and add 50g/2oz of the cheese.
3 Pour the sauce over the leeks and sprinkle with the remaining cheese.
4 Cook on the low rack on combination 200°C/LOW for 10 min, until the cheese is melted and lightly browned.

Cook's note: *If you require the cheese slightly browner, cook for a few minutes on grill combination or under a preheated grill*

Roast potatoes

(serves 4) colour page 115

COMBINATION: 200°C/MEDIUM (50%)

4×15ml/tbsp oil
675g/1½lb potatoes, peeled and cut into pieces

1 Place the oil in a suitable shallow dish and heat on the low rack on combination 200°C/MEDIUM for 5 min.
2 Turn the potatoes in the hot oil and cook for 20–25 min, until well browned. Serve immediately.

Baked Peppers with Sweetcorns and Garlic (above); Courgettes with Basil and Cucumber (above); Leeks au Gratin (above)

Spinach with soured cream and peanuts

(serves 3) colour page 86

MICROWAVE: HIGH (100%)
COMBINATION: 180°C/MEDIUM (50%)

450g/1lb frozen chopped leaf spinach
2×15ml/tbsp peanut butter
150ml/5fl oz soured cream
freshly ground black pepper
50g/2oz dry roasted peanuts

1 Place the spinach in a bowl, cover and cook for 6–8 min on microwave HIGH, until hot. Turn the spinach into a sieve and press out as much liquid as possible.
2 Heat the peanut butter in a bowl for 1 min then add the spinach and stir in the soured cream. Season well with black pepper then add most of the peanuts.
3 Turn into an ovenproof serving dish and scatter with the remaining peanuts. Cook on the low rack on combination 180°C/MEDIUM for 10 min.

Yorkshire pudding

(serves 4)

COMBINATION: 200°C/MEDIUM (50%) and 200°C/LOW (30%)

Yorkshire pudding works well in combination cookers with a continuous microwave power

3×15ml/tbsp oil
1 egg
275ml/10fl oz milk
125g/4oz flour
pinch salt

1 Heat the oil in an ovenproof glass shallow flan dish for 10 min on the low rack on combination 200°C/MEDIUM.
2 Prepare the batter by blending together the egg and milk then adding the flour and a pinch of salt and blending to a smooth batter.
3 Pour the batter into the dish of hot oil and cook on combination 200°C/LOW for 20–25 min.

Cook's note: *If the oven has already been used to cook roast beef and roast potatoes, the oil will require only 6 min at combination 200°C/MEDIUM to heat before adding the batter*

Baked potatoes

(serves 4) colour page 39

COMBINATION: 200°C/MEDIUM (50%)

Serve baked potatoes filled as a supper dish, or topped with butter or soured cream as an accompaniment to meat, fish or vegetarian dishes. If you are cooking another dish for the same meal in the combination oven, cook the baked potatoes first then keep warm in the conventional oven until required. This will help to further crisp the skins of the potatoes

4 large potatoes, approx 225g/8oz each
butter to serve

1 Scrub the potatoes and score the skins with a sharp knife. Place the potatoes on the low rack and cook for 25–28 min on combination 200°C/MEDIUM.
2 Test the potatoes with a skewer – the skins should be crispy and the potato should offer no resistance to the skewer.
3 Slit and serve with butter.

Braised okra with lime pickle

(serves 3–4) colour page 43

MICROWAVE: HIGH (100%)
COMBINATION: 180°C/MEDIUM (50%)

An unusual Indian side dish, the okra or 'ladies fingers' are braised in tea

25g/1oz ghee or butter
1 large onion, sliced
2 cloves garlic, crushed
1×15ml/tbsp ground coriander
1×15ml/tbsp coriander seeds
4 cloves
6 black peppercorns
2 bay leaves
225g/8oz okra, washed and trimmed
½×5ml/tsp salt
1×5ml/tsp indian tea
275ml/10fl oz boiling water
1–2×15ml/tbsp lime pickle
1–2×5ml/tsp sugar, optional

for garnish: chopped coriander leaves

1 Heat the ghee or butter for 1–2 min on microwave HIGH until melted. Add the onion, garlic and ground coriander. Grind the coriander seeds with the cloves and peppercorns and add them to the dish. Add the bay leaves. Cover and cook for 4 min, stirring once.

Desserts and puddings

Above: Mixed Fruit Flan (page 96)
below left: Apricot Frangipan (page 100)
below: Chocolate Roulade (page 97)
right: Clafouti (page 97)

Desserts and puddings

Chocolate and banana choux gâteau

(serves 8)

MICROWAVE: MEDIUM (50%) and HIGH (100%)
COMBINATION: 200°C/LOW (30%)

for the filling:
225g/8oz plain chocolate, broken into small pieces
550ml/1pt milk
50g/2oz cornflour
2 eggs, size 3, separated
25g/1oz caster sugar
2 bananas
1 lemon, juice

for the choux pastry:
75g/3oz butter
275ml/½pt water
150g/5oz plain flour
4 eggs, size 3, beaten

for decoration: whipped cream

1. To make the filling, place the chocolate and three-quarters of the milk into a large bowl. Heat in the microwave on MEDIUM for 4 min or until the milk is hot and the chocolate has melted. Stir halfway through.
2. In another large mixing bowl, blend the cornflour with the egg yolks and the remaining milk. Stir in the caster sugar and the hot, chocolate-flavoured milk. Cook on microwave HIGH for 5–7 min until thickened and boiling, stirring every minute.
3. Whisk the egg whites until very stiff and fold into the hot chocolate mixture a little at a time. Cover the surface with greaseproof paper and cool, then refrigerate until cold.
4. For the choux pastry, place the butter and water into a bowl and heat on HIGH for 4–5 min until the butter is melted and the water is boiling rapidly. Stir halfway through.
5. Add the flour all at once and beat well until the mixture is smooth. Beat in the eggs a little at a time. The mixture will be thick and glossy.
6. Grease and line the base of a 22–25cm/9–10in round cake dish. Place the choux pastry into a piping bag fitted with a large nozzle and pipe concentric rings of pastry over the base of the dish.
7. Place onto the low or recommended rack and cook for 40–50 min on combination 200°C/LOW until well risen and browned. If browning too much, reduce to 180°C/LOW for the last 10–15 min of cooking.
8. Remove from the dish to a cooling rack and make slits in the side of the gâteau to allow some of the steam to escape. Leave until cold then cut the gâteau in half horizontally.
9. Peel and slice the bananas and brush with the lemon juice. Reserve a few of the slices for decoration.
10. Fill the gâteau with the chocolate cream and banana slices. Pipe swirls of whipped cream on the top of the gâteau and decorate with the rest of the slices of banana. Serve straight away.

Mixed fruit flan

(serves 8) *colour page 94*

MICROWAVE: HIGH (100%)
COMBINATION: 200°C/MEDIUM (50%)

Vary the fruit according to what you have available

225g/8oz plain white flour
150g/5oz butter
1×15ml/tbsp icing sugar
1 egg
900–1000g/2–2¼lb mixed prepared dessert fruit, eg strawberries, raspberries, gooseberries, blackberries, pears, apples, bananas, oranges, satsumas, peaches, apricots, plums (see recipe step 3)
few drops lemon juice, optional
275g/10oz redcurrant jelly

1. Place the flour into a mixing bowl with the butter cut into pieces, the icing sugar and egg. Blend all the ingredients together to form a soft dough. Leave to chill for 30 min.
2. Roll the pastry out on a floured surface and carefully line a 25cm/10in flan dish. Prick the base well and bake blind on the low or recommended rack for 13–15 min on combi-

nation 200°C/MEDIUM. Leave to cool.

3 Meanwhile prepare the fruit, leaving soft fruits whole unless large. Leave the skins on the apples if prepared then cut apples, pears and bananas into thick, chunky slices, and brush with a little lemon juice. Divide the oranges so that there are 2–3 segments in each piece, depending on size. Stone, slice, halve or quarter peaches, apricots and plums.
4 Heat the redcurrant jelly for 1 min in the microwave on HIGH and then rub through a sieve. Heap the prepared fruit into the cooled flan case so that the pieces look haphazardly arranged, piling up into a mound in the centre.
5 Brush the fruit liberally with the redcurrant jelly and decorate the flan with fruit leaves if liked before serving.

Apple rum meringue

(serves 6–8)

MICROWAVE: HIGH (100%)
COMBINATION: 180°C/LOW (30%)

100–150g/4–5oz ratafias or macaroons
3–4×15ml/tbsp white rum
675g/1½lb cooking apples, sliced
25g/1oz unsalted butter
25–50g/1–2oz brown sugar, optional
½×5ml/tsp cinnamon
3 egg whites
¼×5ml/tsp salt
175g/6oz caster sugar

1 Arrange the ratafias or macaroons in the base of a 22.5cm/9in flan dish and sprinkle with the rum.
2 Place the apples into a covered bowl or dish with the butter, sugar if used and the cinnamon. Mix well, cover and cook on microwave HIGH for 6–7 min until the apples are just cooked. Leave to cool then spoon over the ratafias.
3 Whisk the egg whites with the salt until stiff, add half the caster sugar and continue whisking until stiff, smooth and glossy. Fold in the remaining sugar.
4 Straight away, spoon the meringue over the apples in the flan dish. Swirl the meringue into soft peaks with a spatula.
5 Cook on combination 180°C/LOW for 9–11 min until the meringue is pale beige. Serve warm or cold with whipped cream if liked.

Clafouti

(serves 6) colour page 95

MICROWAVE: HIGH (100%)
COMBINATION: 200°C/LOW (30%)

A clafouti is a sweet pancake batter cooked with fresh fruit. The dish originates from France and traditionally black cherries are used

675g/1½lb black cherries, fresh or frozen, thawed
3 eggs
3×15ml/tbsp plain flour
pinch salt
5×15ml/tbsp caster sugar
425ml/¾pt milk
1×15ml/tbsp dark rum, optional
25–40g/1–1½oz butter

1 Remove the stones and stalks from the fresh cherries, wash and dry. Drain the thawed frozen fruit thoroughly and remove any stones.
2 Lightly beat the eggs, add the flour and salt, beating thoroughly until smooth then beat in 3×15ml/tbsp of the caster sugar.
3 Heat the milk in the microwave on HIGH until warm and add to the egg and flour mixture with the rum if used.
4 Use some of the butter to grease a large, shallow dish and arrange the cherries in the base. Pour the batter over the cherries and then top with slivers of the remaining butter.
5 Place on the low or recommended rack and cook on combination 200°C/LOW for 17–20 min or until the centre of the batter has set. When cooked, the cherries will rise to the surface and the batter will set like a baked custard.
6 Sprinkle with remaining sugar and serve warm.

Chocolate roulade

(serves 6) colour page 95

COMBINATION: 200°C/LOW (30%)

4 eggs, size 3, separated
100g/4oz plus 1×15ml/tbsp caster sugar
40g/1½oz plain flour
20g/¾oz cocoa
¼×5ml/tsp baking powder
2×5ml/tsp cold water
275ml/½pt double cream
2×15ml/tbsp kirsch

for decoration: chocolate curls, grated chocolate or crushed chocolate flake, and stoned black cherries

1 Whisk the egg yolks with the 100g/4oz caster sugar until very thick. Sift the flour, cocoa and baking powder into the egg yolk mixture then fold in. Mix in the water. Whisk the egg whites until very stiff and carefully fold them, a little at a time, into the cocoa mixture.
2 Pour the sponge mixture into a 24–27cm/9½–10½in square dish which has been lightly greased and the base lined. Cook on the low or recommended rack for 12–15 min on combination 200°C/LOW until well risen and firm to the touch, but do not allow to overcook. Leave to stand for 1 min then turn it onto a sheet of sugared greaseproof paper and allow to cool.
3 Whisk the cream with the kirsch and the remaining sugar until it holds soft peaks. Lightly score across the cake to make rolling easier then spread half the cream over the sponge. Carefully roll up using the paper as a guide.
4 Place the chocolate roll on a flat serving dish and spread over the remaining cream. Mark the cream into swirls, then decorate with chocolate curls. If liked, decorate or serve with stoned black cherries.

Tipsy coffee and praline marble crown

(serves 8–10) colour page 99

MICROWAVE: HIGH (100%)
COMBINATION: 180°C/LOW (30%)

Quick and easy to make, this one-stage mixture is turned into a delicious ring gâteau, filled with a mixture of fresh fruits

for the praline:
40g/1½oz caster sugar
1×15ml/tbsp water
40g/1½oz whole unblanched almonds

for the gâteau:
100g/4oz self-raising flour
½×5ml/tsp baking powder
100g/4oz soft margarine
100g/4oz light soft brown sugar
2 eggs, beaten
1×15ml/tbsp milk
125ml/4fl oz hot water and 3×5ml/tsp instant coffee or 125ml/4fl oz strong black fresh coffee
2×15ml/tbsp coffee liqueur

for serving: mixture of sliced apricot or peach, kiwi fruit, nectarine, strawberries, halved and deseeded grapes

for decoration: double cream, whipped

1 Place the caster sugar for the praline into a bowl with the water and mix together. Heat on microwave HIGH for 10 sec at a time, stirring well in between, until the sugar has dissolved.
2 Add the almonds and cook for 2–3 min until turned to a rich nut brown colour. (Do not leave unattended as the mixture can burn very rapidly.) Turn into a non-stick or lightly oiled tin and leave to cool. Coarsely crush half the praline, finely crush the remainder.
3 Place the flour, baking powder, margarine, sugar, eggs and milk into a large bowl and beat well together until the mixture is blended and smooth. Fold in the finely crushed praline.
4 Turn the mixture into a lightly greased 22–23cm/8½–9in decorative microwave ring mould, smooth the surface and cook on combination 180°C/LOW for 15–18 min until risen and golden brown. Leave to stand for a few minutes and then invert onto a wire rack to cool.
5 Blend the hot water with the instant coffee if used. Mix together the coffee and coffee liqueur. Return the cooled cake to the ring mould and pour over the coffee mixture at intervals around the outside edge to create a marble effect. Leave to soak for 20 min.
6 Turn out onto a serving plate and fill the centre of the ring with the prepared fruits. Pipe some whipped cream around the top edge and sprinkle with the coarsely crushed praline before serving.

Tipsy Coffee and Praline Marble Crown (above); Roast Pheasants with Cranberry and Orange Sauce (page 85)

Blackcurrant and mincemeat lattice tart

(serves 8–10)

COMBINATION: 200°C/MEDIUM (50%) and 200°C/LOW (30%)

The sharpness of the blackcurrants contrasts particularly well with the sweetness of the mincemeat

for the pastry:
275g/10oz plain flour
190g/6½oz butter or margarine
1 egg, size 2

for the filling:
350g/12oz frozen blackcurrants, thawed and drained
400-425g/14–15oz jar mincemeat
2×15ml/tbsp crème de cassis or blackcurrant juice
egg white for brushing
caster sugar for sprinkling

1 Blend together all the ingredients for the pastry to form a soft dough and knead lightly.
2 Cut off two-thirds of the dough, roll out on a lightly floured surface and use to line a 22.5cm/9in flan dish. Bake blind on the low or recommended rack for 8–10 min on combination 200°C/MEDIUM.
3 Gently mix together the blackcurrants, mincemeat and crème de cassis or blackcurrant juice, spoon into the flan case and smooth the surface.
4 Roll out the remaining dough, cut into strips and place over the tart in a lattice arrangement. Brush the pastry lattice strips with egg white and sprinkle with caster sugar.
5 Cook on combination 200°C/LOW for 17–22 min until golden brown. Serve hot or warm with ice cream.

Apricot frangipan

(serves 4–5) *colour page 94*

COMBINATION: 180°C/LOW (30%)

350g/12oz fresh apricots or 425g/15oz can apricot halves
50g/2oz butter or margarine
50g/2oz caster sugar
1 egg
50g/2oz ground almonds
2×15ml/tbsp plain flour
1–2×15ml/tbsp amaretto liqueur, optional
icing sugar for dusting

1 Cut the fresh apricots into halves at the dividing line, twist gently then pull and remove the stones. Drain the canned apricot halves well then pat dry on kitchen paper.
2 Cream the butter or margarine with the caster sugar until soft. Beat in the egg, almonds, flour and liqueur if used, until smooth.
3 Turn the mixture into a lightly buttered or oiled 18–20cm/7–8in shallow microwave cake dish with removable base, or shallow flan dish. Smooth the surface and attractively arrange the apricot halves cut side down, over the top. Cook for 16–20 min on combination 180°C/LOW until light golden brown.
4 Leave to stand for 1–2 min before removing from the cake dish onto a serving plate or serve straight from the flan dish. Dust with icing sugar and serve straight away with whipped cream or vanilla ice cream.

Shoo fly pie

(serves 8)

COMBINATION: 180°C/LOW (30%)

This is a wholewheat version of the traditional dish from America's south, and takes its name from the extreme sweetness which necessitates bees and flies being 'shooed' away

225g/8oz wholewheat flour
pinch salt
100g/4oz sunflower margarine or butter
water for mixing
175g/6oz seedless raisins
75g/3oz soft brown sugar
¼×5ml/tsp bicarbonate of soda

for the topping:
175g/6oz wholewheat flour
¾×5ml/tsp cinnamon
½×5ml/tsp each ground ginger and nutmeg
75g/3oz sunflower margarine or butter
75g/3oz soft brown sugar

1 Make the pastry by placing the flour into a bowl with the salt, rub in the margarine or butter until the mixture resembles breadcrumbs and add sufficient water to make into a soft dough.
2 Roll out on a floured surface and line a 22–23cm/8½–9in flan dish. Prick the base with a fork and sprinkle with the raisins.
3 Mix the sugar with the bicarbonate of soda and 3×15ml/tbsp water and set to one side.

4 Prepare the topping by mixing the flour in a bowl with the spices. Rub in the margarine or butter until the mixture resembles breadcrumbs and stir in the sugar.
5 Pour the sugar and water mixture over the raisins and sprinkle with the topping. Cook on the low or recommended rack for 21–27 min on combination 180°C/LOW until the topping is set and browned. Serve with natural yogurt or cream.

Pears en douillon

(serves 6)

MICROWAVE: HIGH (100%)
COMBINATION: 200°C/MEDIUM (50%)

The pears take a while to prepare but are well worth the effort for their eye-catching appeal and tasty result

350g/12oz frozen puff pastry, thawed
6 firm ripe pears
2×15ml/tbsp sugar
2–3×15ml/tbsp brandy or kirsch, optional
1 egg, beaten
6×15ml/tbsp redcurrant jelly

for decoration: 2.5cm/1in piece angelica, cut into 6 strips

1 Roll out the pastry thinly on a lightly floured surface into an elongated rectangle and cut into long, 1.5cm/½in wide strips. Brush the strips lightly with water.
2 Peel the pears, remove the stalk and cut a thin slice from the base so that the pear stands upright. Using a corer, carefully remove the core from the stalk end; do not cut right through the pear.
3 Fill the holes with a little sugar and brandy or kirsch if used. Keeping the pears upright and leaving the hole at the top free, start from the top and wind the pastry strips around the pears overlapping slightly as you go. Join on another strip when necessary.
4 Roll any remaining pastry thinly and cut into leaves. Attach firmly at the top of the pears with beaten egg, then brush the pastry all over with the egg.
5 Place onto a baking plate on the low or recommended rack and cook on combination 200°C/MEDIUM for 20–25 min until golden brown.
6 Meanwhile sieve the redcurrant jelly. When the pears are cooked, heat the redcurrant jelly on microwave HIGH for 1–2 min until hot, stirring once.
7 Fill the hole in each pear with the redcurrant jelly and place a piece of angelica in the top to resemble a stalk. Serve with whipped cream.

Grape and yogurt torte

(serves 6–8) colour opposite

MICROWAVE: HIGH (100%)
COMBINATION: 180°C/LOW (30%)

A light refreshing dessert

for the almond base:
100g/4oz ground almonds
90g/3½oz caster sugar
50g/2oz fresh breadcrumbs
¾×5ml/tsp baking powder
3 egg whites

for the mousse:
1 sachet powdered gelatine
75ml/3fl oz dry white wine
150ml/¼pt double cream, lightly whipped
150ml/¼pt natural yogurt
2 egg whites
2×15ml/tbsp caster sugar
225g/8oz seedless white grapes, halved

1. For the base, mix together the almonds, sugar, breadcrumbs and baking powder in a bowl. Whisk the egg whites and fold into the dry ingredients carefully with a metal spoon.
2. Turn the mixture into a lightly greased 20cm/8in microwave cake dish with removable base, and smooth the surface. Cook on combination 180°C/LOW for 11–14 min until firm and lightly browned. Leave to cool in the dish.
3. For the topping, sprinkle the gelatine onto the wine and leave to soak for a few minutes. Heat on microwave HIGH for 15–30 sec until hot then stir until dissolved.
4. Gently stir the cream with the yogurt to blend and fold in the gelatine.
5. Whisk the egg whites with the caster sugar until holding soft peaks and fold into the cream and yogurt mixture which will have begun to set. Fold in half the grapes.
6. Turn the mixture into the dish on top of the almond base, mounding it up in the middle if necessary. (It does not matter if the base has slightly shrunk from the edges of the dish.) Smooth the surface and leave to chill for 1–2 hr until set.
7. Carefully remove the torte from the dish onto a serving plate and arrange concentric circles of the remaining grapes on the top of the mousse. Serve cold.

Cook's note: *Other fruit could be substituted such as apricots or mandarins*

St Clementine's Cheesecake

(serves 8–10) colour opposite

COMBINATION: 200°C/LOW (30%)

for the base:
225g/8oz wheatmeal or digestive biscuits, crushed
100g/4oz soft brown sugar
1×5ml/tsp ground cinnamon, optional
100g/4oz butter, melted

for the filling:
225g/8oz curd or ricotta cheese
225g/8oz cream cheese
100g/4oz caster sugar
1 lemon, finely grated rind and 1×5ml/tsp juice
1 orange, finely grated rind and 1×5ml/tsp juice
3 eggs, separated
3×15ml/tbsp cornflour
150ml/¼pt natural yogurt

for decoration: thin slices of lemon and orange and icing sugar, optional

1. Mix the biscuit crumbs with the sugar, cinnamon if used, and melted butter until well blended and press into the base of a lightly greased 27cm/10½in flan dish.
2. Beat the cheeses with the caster sugar, lemon and orange rinds and juice, egg yolks and cornflour until smooth.
3. Whisk the egg whites until they hold stiff peaks. Gently fold the yogurt into the cheese mixture, followed by the egg whites, using a large, metal spoon.
4. Pour the mixture over the biscuit base in the flan dish and smooth the surface. Cook on the low or recommended baking rack for 20–25 min on combination 200°C/LOW or until set and lightly browned. Leave to cool.
5. When cold, decorate with thin slices (or shapes cut from slices) of lemon and orange and dust with icing sugar if used, before serving.

St Clementine's Cheesecake (above); Grape and Yogurt Torte (above)

Syrup and Almond Flan

(serves 8–10)

COMBINATION: 200°C/MEDIUM (50%) and 180°C/LOW (30%)
MICROWAVE: MEDIUM (50%)

For the pastry:
275g/10oz plain flour, half white and half wholewheat if preferred
190g/6½oz butter or margarine
1 egg, size 2

for the filling:
225g/8oz golden syrup
100g/4oz soft light brown sugar
50g/2oz butter or margarine
175g/6oz fresh breadcrumbs
1 lemon, juice and grated rind
2 eggs, beaten
150ml/¼pt milk
175g/6oz flaked almonds

1 Blend together all the ingredients for the pastry and knead lightly to form a soft dough. Roll out on a lightly floured surface and use to line a 28cm/11in flan dish.
2 Prick the pastry case well with a fork then bake blind on the low or recommended rack for 12 min on combination 200°C/MEDIUM. Leave to cool.
3 Place the syrup, sugar and butter or margarine into a bowl and heat in the microwave on MEDIUM for 5 min until hot, then stir to blend. Add the breadcrumbs, lemon juice and rind, eggs, milk and 100g/4oz of the almonds. Mix well together.
4 Pour the mixture into the flan case and smooth the surface. Sprinkle with the remaining almonds and cook on combination 180°C/LOW for 21–26 min until light golden brown.
5 Allow to stand for a few minutes before serving warm with cream.

Oat plum crumble

(serves 4–6)

MICROWAVE: MEDIUM (50%)
COMBINATION: 200°C/MEDIUM (50%)

The delicious flapjack-type topping contrasts particularly well with plums. Other fruit such as greengages or damsons could also be used

75g/3oz golden syrup
50g/2oz flaked almonds
75g/3oz butter or margarine
1×5ml/tsp ground ginger
175g/6oz rolled oats
900g/2lb ripe plums

1 Measure the syrup into a bowl with the almonds, butter and ginger. Heat in the microwave on MEDIUM for 3 min until the butter has melted.
2 Stir to blend the ingredients, then stir in the oats and mix well to ensure they are coated with the syrup mixture.
3 Halve and stone the plums and arrange them in the base of a shallow casserole dish. Sprinkle with the oat mixture and lightly smooth the surface.
4 Bake on the low or recommended rack on combination 200°C/MEDIUM for 12–15 min until the topping is browned and crisp and the plums are tender.

Mille-feuilles dessert cake

(serves 8)

MICROWAVE: MEDIUM/HIGH (70%)
COMBINATION: 200°C/MEDIUM (50%) and 200°C/HIGH (100%)

550g/1lb frozen puff pastry, thawed

for the pastry cream:
3 egg yolks
250ml/9fl oz milk
2×15ml/tbsp caster sugar
3×15ml/tbsp cornflour
1–2×15ml/tbsp brandy
150ml/¼pt double cream, whipped

for decoration:
75g/3oz chopped almonds, apricot jam, warmed icing sugar for dusting

1 Cut the puff pastry into 2×225g/8oz pieces. Roll out each piece on a lightly floured surface and cut into 2×20–22.5cm/8–9in diameter rounds. Place each round onto a dampened baking plate and cook one at a time on combination 200°C/MEDIUM for 9–10 min until well risen and light golden brown. If placing the second one into a hot oven, reduce the second cooking time to 7–8 min. Alternatively, if cooking on two levels at the same time, cook for 12–13 min and be prepared to swop shelf positions or remove the top round first. Otherwise, cook both together on two levels by convection for 18–22 min.
2 Remove the pastry to a cooling rack and leave until cold. Split each round into half horizontally and if necessary, trim the rounds to an even circle. Press them down lightly.
3 For the pastry cream, whisk together the egg yolks, milk, sugar and cornflour until smooth. Heat in the microwave on MEDIUM/HIGH for 3–4 min until thickened, whisking every minute. Do not allow to boil. Stir while cooling and flavour with the brandy. When cold, fold in the whipped double cream.
4 Brown the chopped almonds on a baking plate for 3–6 min on combination 200°C/HIGH until lightly toasted (use a grill combination if your cooker has this facility). Leave to cool.
5 Place the pastry rounds on top of each other with the pastry cream in between.
6 Carefully spread the warm jam around the edge of the cake and gently press on most of the toasted chopped almonds. Dust the top of the cake liberally with icing sugar and sprinkle with the remaining almonds.

Sweet pear flan

(serves 6)

COMBINATION: 180°C/LOW (30%)

Round pears such as Comice are best for this dish as they fan out nicely to fit the pastry case

for the pâté sucrée:
175g/6oz plain white flour
75g/3oz butter, cut into pieces
3 egg yolks
50g/2oz caster sugar

for the filling:
50g/2oz cream cheese or low fat soft cheese
1 egg
2×15ml/tbsp milk
1–2×15ml/tbsp kirsch
25g/1oz demerara sugar plus 1–1½×15ml/tbsp
pinch grated nutmeg
3 even-sized pears
1×15ml/tbsp dried wholewheat breadcrumbs

1 Place the flour on a work surface and make a well in the centre. Add the butter to the well with the egg yolks and the caster sugar. Work the mixture together by 'pinching' with the fingertips, then knead lightly. Alternatively, place all the ingredients into a food processor and blend quickly together until smooth. Wrap and chill for about 30 min.
2 Roll out the pastry quite thickly and line a suitable 22cm/8½in flan dish. Prick the base well with a fork and bake blind on the low or recommended baking rack for 10 min on combination 180°C/LOW until just cooked. Allow to cool slightly.
3 For the filling, beat the cream cheese until soft, then beat in the egg, milk, kirsch, 25g/1oz demerara sugar and the nutmeg.
4 Peel the pears, cut into halves lengthwise and scoop out the cores. Thinly slice each half either lengthwise or crosswise and carefully place into the flan case, narrow ends to the centre. Fan out the slices to fit attractively.
5 Spoon the custard over the pears into the flan case and sprinkle with the rest of the demerara sugar and the breadcrumbs.
6 Place onto the low or recommended rack and cook for 16–17 min until the custard has set. Serve warm.

Baking

Above: Gingerbread (page 113); below left: Banana Nut Teabread (page 117) centre: Chelsea Buns (page 108) right: Passion Cake (page 108)

Baking

Passion cake

(makes 1 large cake) colour page 107

MICROWAVE: MEDIUM (50%)
COMBINATION: 160°C/LOW (30%)

150g/5oz butter or margarine
200g/7oz soft brown sugar
2 eggs, beaten
200g/7oz self-raising flour
3×5ml/tsp baking powder
pinch salt
1×5ml/tsp ground cinnamon
½×5ml/tsp grated nutmeg
50g/2oz walnuts, chopped
50g/2oz sultanas
175g/6oz carrots, finely grated
1–2×15ml/tbsp milk
icing sugar for dusting

for the frosting:
225g/8oz cream cheese
40g/1½oz icing sugar, sifted
1×15ml/tbsp lemon juice

for decoration: grated carrot or walnut halves

1. Grease a 20cm/8in round cake dish and line the base with a circle of baking parchment or lightly greased greaseproof paper.
2. Melt the butter in the microwave for 2–3 min on MEDIUM. Beat in the sugar and eggs.
3. Sift the flour, baking powder, salt and spices and fold into the egg and sugar mixture. Finally fold in the walnuts, sultanas, grated carrots and a little milk to make a soft dropping consistency.
4. Turn the mixture into the prepared dish and cook on the low or recommended rack on combination 160°C/LOW for 25–30 min. Test the cake with a skewer inserted into the centre – if cooked, the skewer will come out clean. Leave in the dish for a few minutes before removing to a cooling rack.
5. When cold, dust the cake with icing sugar or coat the cake with cream cheese frosting – made by creaming the cheese with the icing sugar and lemon juice until smooth – and decorate with grated carrot or walnut halves.

Chelsea buns

(makes 10–12) colour page 106

MICROWAVE: HIGH (100%)
COMBINATION: 200°C/LOW (30%)

for the yeast dough:
15g/½oz fresh yeast or 1½×5ml/tsp dried yeast
½×5ml/tsp caster sugar
125ml/4fl oz milk
225g/8oz plain flour
½×5ml/tsp salt
20g/¾oz butter or margarine
1 egg, beaten

for the filling:
25g/1oz butter or margarine
150g/5oz currants
50g/2oz soft brown sugar and
  some for sprinkling
melted butter for brushing
pinch cinnamon or mixed spice
caster sugar, optional

1. Lightly grease a large shallow round or square dish and line the base with baking parchment or greased greaseproof paper.
2. Place the yeast in a small bowl with the sugar. Heat the milk in the microwave on HIGH for 20–30 sec until warm and pour onto the yeast and sugar. Leave until frothy.
3. Sift the flour and salt into a bowl and rub in the butter or margarine. Add the yeast and milk mixture with the egg and beat to form a soft dough. Knead thoroughly until smooth and elastic then cover and leave to prove until double in size.
4. Knock back the dough and roll out on a lightly floured surface into an oblong measuring about 30×22cm/12×9in.
5. For the filling, melt the butter or margarine in the microwave on HIGH for 1 min and brush over the dough. Sprinkle with the currants and 50g/2oz soft brown sugar.
6. Roll up from the long side like a swiss roll and cut into 2.5cm/1in slices with a sharp knife. Place the slices, cut side down, around the edge and in the centre of the prepared dish.

7 Brush liberally with melted butter, sprinkle with the sugar and cinnamon or mixed spice. Cover and leave to prove as before until double in size.
8 Place on the low or recommended rack and cook on combination 200°C/LOW for 14–18 min until golden brown.
9 Leave to stand for a few minutes before removing to a cooling rack. Sprinkle lightly with caster sugar if wished.

Spiced loaf

(makes 1 small loaf) colour page 111

MICROWAVE: HIGH (100%)
COMBINATION: 200°C/LOW (30%)

A delicious, quick-to-make bread using easy-blend dried yeast

325g/11oz strong plain flour
1×5ml/tsp cumin or caraway seeds
1×5ml/tsp ground coriander
1×5ml/tsp salt
¼×5ml/tsp pepper
1 sachet easy-blend dried yeast
150ml/¼pt milk
25g/1oz butter or margarine, softened
1 egg, beaten
few cumin or caraway and coriander seeds for sprinkling

1 Place the flour into a bowl with the 1×5ml/tsp cumin or caraway seeds, the ground coriander, salt and pepper. Stir in the easy-blend dried yeast.
2 Heat the milk in the microwave for 30–45 sec on HIGH until lukewarm. Add the milk to the flour with the butter or margarine and most of the egg, saving a little for brushing.
3 Mix the ingredients together to form a dough then knead thoroughly until smooth. Form into an oval and place onto a lightly oiled suitable baking dish or plate. Cover and leave to rise in a warm place for about 30 min until doubled in size.
4 Slash the top of the dough with a sharp knife, brush with the remaining beaten egg and sprinkle with a few seeds.
5 Bake on the low or recommended rack for 16–18 min on combination 200°C/LOW. Transfer to a wire rack to cool. Serve sliced and buttered.

Whisked sponge

(cuts into 8)

COMBINATION: 220°C/LOW (30%)

A light sponge cake which relies on the whisking of air into the eggs as the raising agent, best eaten on the day it is made

4 eggs
100g/4oz caster sugar
100g/4oz plain flour
pinch salt
jam
whipped cream
icing sugar

1 Lightly grease a 19–20cm/7½–8in cake dish and line the base with a circle of baking parchment or greaseproof paper. Preheat the oven on convection mode to 220°C if not already hot from previous cooking.
2 Whisk the eggs and sugar together until trebled in volume and really thick and creamy. It is ready when a trail of the mixture can be held on the surface for at least 5 sec.
3 Sift the flour and salt and sprinkle over the mixture, very carefully folding in with a metal spoon or spatula and turning the mixture over from the base of the bowl to ensure that all the flour is mixed in.
4 Pour into the prepared container and cook on the low or recommended rack on combination 220°C/LOW for 9–11 min until well risen and pale golden in colour. Leave for a few minutes before removing to a cooling rack.
5 When cold, cut in half horizontally and sandwich the halves together with jam and cream. Dust the top with icing sugar.

Genoese sponge

(cuts into 8)

MICROWAVE: HIGH (100%)
COMBINATION: 200°C/LOW (30%)

This cake has better keeping qualities than the whisked sponge and makes a good base for various fillings and toppings for gâteaux

Follow the ingredients and recipe points 1 and 2 for whisked sponge above.
3 Melt 50g/2oz butter or margarine on microwave HIGH for 1–1½ min and add to the

thickened mixture with the flour by pouring it in a thin stream down the side of the bowl while folding in the flour and butter with a metal spoon or spatula. Fold in very carefully, ensuring that the spoon cuts across the base of the bowl so that all the flour and butter are well mixed in.

4 Cook on combination 200°C/LOW, for 9–11 min.
5 Decorate as for whisked sponge.

Salami bread

(makes 1 large loaf) colour opposite

COMBINATION: 200°C/LOW (30%)

375g/13oz strong plain flour
150g/5oz rye flour
1½×5ml/tsp salt
1 sachet easy-blend dried yeast
1–1½×15ml/tbsp finely chopped parsley
275ml/½pt lukewarm water, approx
1 small onion, finely chopped
40–50g/1½–2oz cheese, finely diced
75–90g/3–3½oz salami, finely diced
1×15ml/tbsp coarse sea-salt
1×15ml/tbsp plain flour

1 Place the strong plain and rye flours, salt, yeast and parsley into a large bowl and mix together. Stir in sufficient lukewarm water to form a soft dough and knead well.
2 Work the onion, cheese and salami into the kneaded dough until evenly distributed. Knead on a lightly floured surface and form into a flattish, round shape.
3 Place onto a greased baking plate. Cover with greased polythene and leave in a warm place to rise. This will take about 50–60 min.
4 Cut a diamond pattern over the top of the loaf using a sharp knife. Brush with water and sprinkle with sea-salt mixed with the flour.
5 Cook on the low or recommended rack for 18–23 min on combination 200°C/LOW until well risen and golden brown. Turn onto a wire rack to cool. Serve sliced and buttered as a snack or part of a buffet or picnic.

Cook's note: *Vary the ingredients to give alternative interesting flavours. All kinds of sausage, cooked bacon or ham can replace the salami and be added to the same basic dough. A little chopped red and green pepper will give a colourful loaf*

Sesame ball loaf

(makes 12 rolls) colour opposite

COMBINATION: 200°C/LOW (30%)

450g/1lb plain flour
1–2×15ml/tbsp caster sugar
1×5ml/tsp salt
1 sachet easy-blend dried yeast
25g/1oz butter or margarine, softened
1 egg, lightly beaten
225ml/8fl oz lukewarm water
melted butter for brushing
2×15ml/tbsp sesame seeds

1 Lightly butter a 19–20cm/7½–8in round, shallow dish and line the base with a circle of baking parchment or greased greaseproof paper.
2 Place the flour, caster sugar, salt and yeast into a bowl and mix well together. Add the butter or margarine, egg and water and beat vigorously until smooth and a soft dough is formed. Knead well, then cover and leave to rise in a warm place, about 45 min.
3 Knock back the dough and form into a sausage. Cut into 12 evenly sized pieces. Knead each piece and place into the prepared dish, 8 balls around the outside and 4 in the centre.
4 Brush with melted butter and sprinkle with the sesame seeds. Cover and prove again until well risen, about 30 min.
5 Place the dish onto the low or recommended rack. Cook on combination 200°C/LOW for 15–20 min until risen and golden brown. Leave in the dish for a few minutes before removing to a cooling rack. Serve broken into rolls with butter.

Variation

Plaited loaf

Follow the above recipe to step 3. Form the dough into a sausage and cut into 3 lengthwise. Shape each piece into a sausage and plait the 3 together. Place onto a greased baking plate and follow steps 4 and 5 above.

From back: Sesame Ball Loaf (above); Salami Bread (above); Spiced Loaf (page 109)

Madeira Cake

(cuts into 10–12 wedges)

COMBINATION: 180°C/LOW (30%)

175g/6oz butter or margarine
175g/6oz caster sugar
1 lemon, grated rind
3 eggs
100g/4oz plain flour
100g/4oz self-raising flour
pinch salt
2 × 15ml/tbsp milk
1 or 2 slices candid lemon peel

1 Lightly grease a 18–19cm/7–7½in cake dish and line the base with baking parchment or lightly greased greaseproof paper.
2 Cream together the butter or margarine, caster sugar and lemon rind until light and fluffy.
3 Beat in the eggs a little at a time. Sieve the flours and salt, and fold into the creamed mixture. Finally fold in the milk.
4 Turn the mixture into the prepared dish, smooth the surface and place the lemon peel on the top in the centre.
5 Place on the low or recommended rack and cook for 20–25 min until risen and golden brown. Leave to stand for 10–15 min before removing the cake from the dish to a wire rack to cool.

Variations

Fruit cake
Omit the lemon rind and candied peel and fold in 175g/6oz mixed dried fruit, 25g/1oz chopped peel and 25g/1oz chopped glacé cherries to the mixture after adding the flour.

Cherry cake
Omit the lemon rind and candied peel. Add a few drops of vanilla or almond essence to the creamed mixture then fold in 175g/6oz chopped glacé cherries after adding the flour.

Hazelnut
Omit the lemon rind and candied peel. Add a few drops of vanilla essence to the creamed mixture and fold in 100g/4oz chopped, toasted hazelnuts with the flour.

Victoria Sandwich

(cuts into 8–10 wedges)

COMBINATION: 180°C/LOW (30%)

Quick to make, this recipe uses a one-stage mixture

175g/6oz soft margarine
175g/6oz caster sugar
3 eggs
175g/6oz self-raising flour
½ × 5ml/tsp baking powder
pinch salt

1 Lightly oil a 18–19cm/7–7½in cake dish and line the base with a circle of baking parchment or lightly oiled greaseproof paper.

2 Place all the ingredients into a mixing bowl and beat together until smooth and light in texture.
3 Turn the mixture into the prepared dish and smooth the surface. Place on the low or recommended rack and cook for 14–16 min until well risen and golden.
4 Allow to stand for a few minutes before removing from the dish. Leave until cool before cutting in half horizontally. Sandwich the halves together with a filling of your choice.

Gingerbread

(makes 1 large cake) colour page 106

MICROWAVE: HIGH (100%)
COMBINATION: 160°C/LOW (30%)

This black sticky gingerbread is best left to mature for 2–3 days before serving

100g/4oz butter or margarine
225g/8oz black treacle
75g/3oz soft brown sugar
2×15ml/tbsp orange marmalade
150ml/¼pt milk
½×5ml/tsp bicarbonate of soda
100g/4oz self-raising flour
100g/4oz wholemeal flour
2×5ml/tsp ground ginger
1×5ml/tsp mixed spice
2 eggs, beaten

for serving: whipped double cream, optional

1 Lightly grease a 20cm/8in cake dish and line the base.
2 Place the butter or margarine, treacle, sugar and marmalade into a bowl and melt in the microwave on HIGH for 2 min. Stir well together.
3 Heat the milk for 30 sec and add the bicarbonate of soda.
4 Stir together the flours and spices in a large bowl. Beat in the butter and treacle mixture until smooth then beat in the eggs and milk.
5 Pour the mixture into the prepared dish and place on the low or recommended rack.
6 Cook on combination 160°C/LOW for 23–28 min until risen and firm. Leave in the dish for a few minutes before removing to a cooling rack.
7 If liked, before serving cut the cake horizontally into 5–6 layers and sandwich together with thin layers of whipped double cream.

Country bread

(makes one large loaf)

COMBINATION: 200°C/LOW (30%)

175g/6oz strong plain flour
175g/6oz wholewheat flour
175g/6oz rye flour
2×5ml/tsp salt
1 sachet easy-blend dried yeast
2×15ml/tbsp oil
350ml/12fl oz lukewarm water, approximately
rye flour for sprinkling

1 Place all the flours into a large mixing bowl with the salt and yeast. Mix the oil with the water and add sufficient to the flour mixture to make a soft dough.
2 Mix well together and knead lightly. Turn onto a floured surface and knead to form an oblong shape. Place onto a baking plate, cover and leave to rise for about 50–60 min.
3 When well risen, brush with water and cut slashes on the top with a sharp knife. Sprinkle with rye flour.
4 Place onto a low or recommended rack and cook for 18–23 min until risen and golden brown. Turn the loaf over for the last 5 min cooking time if required.
5 Leave the loaf to cool on a wire rack, covered with a cloth if a soft crust is preferred.

Shortbread

(makes 12 pieces) colour page 55

COMBINATION: 160°C/LOW (30%)

225g/8oz flour
60g/2oz caster sugar
160g/5oz butter or margarine
caster sugar for dusting

1 Lightly oil a 20cm/8in shallow glass dish and line with baking parchment.
2 Mix together the flour and sugar then rub in the butter or margarine, bringing the mixture together into a ball.
3 Press the shortbread into the prepared dish and spread evenly using the back of a metal spoon. Mark into portions and prick well with a fork.
4 Cook on the low rack on combination 160°C/LOW for 13–15 min, until golden brown. Mark into pieces, sprinkle with caster sugar and allow to cool. Remove from the dish when cold.

Christmas cake

(makes 1×19cm/7½in cake) colour opposite

COMBINATION: 160°C/LOW (30%)

This recipe may be used for any rich fruit cake

175g/6oz sultanas
175g/6oz stoned raisins
225g/8oz currants
75g/3oz mixed peel, chopped
75g/3oz glacé cherries, halved
25g/1oz ground almonds
25g/1oz blanched almonds, chopped
3–4×15ml/tbsp sherry, ale or milk
3–4×15ml/tbsp lemon or orange juice
few drops each almond and vanilla essence, optional
165g/5½oz butter
165g/5½oz soft brown sugar
½ lemon, grated rind
½ orange, grated rind
3 eggs, beaten
1×15ml/tbsp black treacle
175g/6oz plain flour
½×5ml/tsp each ground nutmeg, ginger and cinnamon
¼×5ml/tsp salt

1. Place all the prepared fruits and nuts into a bowl and mix well together. Stir in the liquid ingredients and essences if used and leave to stand for about 1 hr.
2. Cream the butter and sugar with the lemon and orange rinds until light and fluffy. Beat in the eggs then stir in the black treacle.
3. Sift the flour with the spices and salt and fold into the creamed mixture alternatively with the fruits. Add a little extra liquid if necessary to give a medium dropping consistency.
4. Spoon the mixture into a 19cm/7½in cake dish which has been lightly greased and the base lined. Smooth the top and slightly hollow out the centre of the cake.
5. Cook for 40–50 min on combination 160°C/LOW, testing after minimum time with a skewer inserted into the centre of the cake – if cooked it will come out clean.
6. Leave the cake to cool before turning out of the dish. To store, wrap the cake in fresh greaseproof paper and then completely in foil. A small amount of brandy or sherry can be brushed over the top and sides of the cake at regular intervals during storage.

Oatmeal soda bread

(makes 1 loaf)

COMBINATION: 200°C/LOW (30%)

Unlike loaves made with yeast, soda bread requires very little kneading – just sufficient to bind the dough together – and no proving time. Although it will successfully freeze, it is best eaten when fresh

400g/14oz plain wheatmeal flour
175g/6oz medium oatmeal
2×5ml/tsp bicarbonate of soda
2×5ml/tsp cream of tartar
1×5ml/tsp salt
150ml/¼pt natural yogurt
cold water
2×15ml/tbsp oil
3×15ml/tbsp wholegrain mustard
1 egg yolk

1. Place the flour, oatmeal, bicarbonate of soda, cream of tartar and salt into a bowl and stir together.
2. Place the yogurt into a measuring jug and make up to 325ml/11fl oz with cold water. Whisk lightly to blend and then beat in the oil and 2×15ml/tbsp of the mustard.
3. Add the liquid to the dry ingredients and mix to a soft dough, adding a drop more cold water if necessary. Knead lightly on a floured surface until smooth.
4. Shape the dough into a round measuring about 15cm/6in in diameter and 4cm/1½in deep and make shallow slashes across the top with a sharp knife.
5. Place the dough onto a suitable baking tray/dish which has been lightly dusted with a little wholewheat flour.
6. Cook on the low or recommended rack for 14–18 min on combination 200°C/LOW until risen and golden brown. Meanwhile, blend the egg yolk with the remaining 1×15ml/tbsp of the mustard.
7. Brush the surface of the bread with the egg yolk mixture and bake for a further 3–5 min until well glazed. Transfer to a cooling rack and eat warm or cold cut into slices.

Honey Roast Gammon (page 40); Roast Potatoes (page 90); Brussels Sprouts with Stilton and Walnut Sauce (page 89); Christmas Turkey Galantine (page 36); Christmas Cake (above)

Wholewheat scone round

(cuts into 8)

COMBINATION: 200°C/LOW (30%)

This scone round is very quick to make but is better if placed into a hot oven, so bake after cooking another dish while the oven is still hot or preheat for 10 min

225g/8oz wholewheat flour
½×5ml/tsp salt
1×5ml/tsp bicarbonate of soda
1×5ml/tsp cream of tartar
50g/2oz butter or margarine
150ml/¼pt milk, yogurt or buttermilk, approximately

1 Preheat the oven in the convection mode to 200°C for 10 min. (See step 5 and cook's note below.)
2 Place flour, salt, bicarbonate of soda and cream of tartar into a mixing bowl. Add the butter or margarine and rub into the flour until the mixture resembles fine breadcrumbs.
3 Add sufficient of the liquid to mix to a soft dough. Turn onto a floured surface and knead lightly until well mixed.
4 Roll or pat out to a round about 18cm/7in in diameter and place onto a lightly greased baking plate. Mark into 8 wedges by scoring to the depth of about 12mm/½in with a sharp knife.
5 Change to the combination mode 200°C/LOW and cook on the low or recommended rack for 8–10 min until risen and lightly browned. Turn onto a wire rack to cool. Serve warm, split and buttered.

Variations

Fruit wholewheat scone round
Stir in 50g/2oz mixed dried fruit and 25g/1oz soft brown or caster sugar to the rubbed-in mixture before adding sufficient liquid to mix.

Cheese wholewheat scone round
Finely grate 50g/2oz strong cheddar cheese and mix 40g/1½oz in to the rubbed-in mixture before adding sufficient liquid to mix. Sprinkle the remaining cheese over the top of the scone round before baking.

Cook's note: *If preferred, cook on convection only from cold for 18–23 min*

Flapjack

(makes 12 pieces)

MICROWAVE: HIGH (100%) and MEDIUM (50%)
COMBINATION: 200°C/LOW (30%)

This recipe uses the microwave to melt the butter and sugar for the flapjack without danger of it burning, then combines with traditional heating for a rapidly baked result

175g/6oz margarine or butter
175g/6oz demerara sugar
250g/9oz rolled oats

1 Lightly grease a 20cm/8in round glass dish and line with baking parchment.
2 Cut the margarine or butter into pieces and melt on microwave HIGH for 2–3 min. Add the demerara sugar, stir well then heat for 4–5 min on microwave MEDIUM, until the sugar is dissolved.
3 Stir in the oats and mix thoroughly.
4 Turn into the prepared dish and smooth the surface with the back of a metal spoon.
5 Bake on combination 200°C/LOW for 7–8 min, until pale golden brown. Mark into portions while still hot, then allow to cool.
6 Cut when cold, and store in an air-tight tin.

Banana nut teabread

(makes 1 large loaf) *colour page 106*

COMBINATION: 160°C/LOW (30%)

This is a very good way of using up ripe bananas which give a fragrant taste and a deliciously moist consistency to the loaf

100g/4oz butter or margarine
150g/5oz soft brown sugar
2 eggs, lightly beaten
3 medium-sized ripe bananas, mashed
225g/8oz plain flour
3×5ml/tsp baking powder
½×5ml/tsp salt
good pinch nutmeg
50–75g/2–3oz walnuts or hazelnuts, chopped

1 Lightly grease a 900g/2lb loaf dish and line the base with baking parchment or greased greaseproof paper.
2 Cream together the butter or margarine and sugar until light and fluffy. Beat in the eggs a little at a time then add the mashed bananas.
3 Sieve together the flour, baking powder, salt and nutmeg and fold into the creamed mixture with the nuts.
4 Pour the mixture into the prepared dish and place on the low or recommended rack. Cook for 25–35 min on combination 160°C/LOW. Leave in the dish for 10 min before turning out onto a wire rack to cool.
5 Serve sliced, either plain or buttered.

Granary loaf

(makes one medium-size loaf)

COMBINATION: 200°C/LOW (30%)

450g/1lb granary flour
2×5ml/tsp salt
1 sachet easy-blend dried yeast
2×15ml/tbsp oil
lukewarm water

1 Place the granary flour into a large mixing bowl. Add the salt and yeast and mix together.
2 Measure the oil into a measuring jug and add lukewarm water to make 275ml/½pt.
3 Add to the flour and mix to a elastic dough. Knead well then cover and leave to prove until double in size.
4 Knock back the dough and shape into a deep round. Place onto a greased baking plate and leave to rise again.
5 Place onto the low or recommended rack and cook for 15–20 min on combination 200°C/LOW until well risen and golden brown. Transfer to a wire rack until cool.

Variations

White bread dough
Substitute 450g/1lb strong white flour for the granary flour.
Wholewheat loaf
Substitute either 225g/8oz each strong white flour and wholewheat flour, or 450g/1lb wholewheat flour, for the granary flour.

Carob and peanut cake

(cuts into 12)

MICROWAVE: HIGH (100%)
COMBINATION: 180°C/LOW (30%)

This cake combines the popular wholefood ingredients of carob powder, peanuts, and honey to make an alternative to chocolate cake

175g/6oz butter or margarine
450g/1lb clear honey
75g/3oz carob powder
250g/9oz self-raising wholewheat flour
pinch salt
2 eggs, beaten
1×5ml/tsp vanilla essence
175g/6oz shelled peanuts

1 Lightly grease and line the base of a suitable deep 20cm/8in round dish.
2 Place the butter or margarine in a bowl and heat on microwave HIGH for 2 min, or until melted. Add the honey and carob powder and beat well.
3 Stir the flour and salt into the bowl then add the eggs and vanilla essence. Beat well, then add the peanuts.
4 Spoon the mixture into the prepared dish and cook on combination 180°C/LOW for 20 min, until a skewer inserted into the cake comes out clean.
5 Allow to cool for 5–10 min then turn out onto a wire rack and allow to cool completely.

Acknowledgements

Combination cookers from the following companies were used in the test and research work for this book:

Belling and Company Limited
Hitachi
Hotpoint Limited
Jones and Brother Limited
Panasonic UK Limited
Sanyo Marubeni Limited
Sharp Electronics Limited
Siemens Domestic Appliances
Tricity Domestic Appliances

Food prepared for photography by Rosemary Moon, assisted by Jane Abbey

Photography, planning and props by John Plimmer, RPM Photographic, 10 The Pallant, Havant, Hants

Line illustrations by Mona Thorogood

Index

Index